Johnny's Kingdom

First published in 2002 by: B.E.P.P. Ltd, Temple Way, Bristol, BS99 7HD
in conjunction with Hochland Communications Ltd, The Precinct Centre,
Oxford Road, Manchester M13 9QA.

Text: © 2002 Christina Zaba, Johnny Kingdom and the Western Daily Press.
Images: © 2002 Johnny Kingdom unless otherwise stated.

Additional photography by: Tony Freeman, Jonathan Hawes, Steven Govier,
Steve Guscott, Richard Taylor-Jones, Western Daily Press picture library.

Artwork by: Indi Davies

Designed by: Gwilym Hughes

Some of the material in this book has previously been published
in the Western Daily Press.

Some of the images in this book were transferred from broadcast film
to print format in the studios and Graphics department of HTV West.

The television series 'Johnny Kingdom's Wild West' was produced by
Available Light Productions for HTV.

ISBN: 1-904038-06-9

Printed in Great Britain by IMPS Ltd.

Johnny's Kingdom

The secret world of Exmoor

by

Johnny Kingdom

with Christina Zaba

WESTERN
Daily Press

Dedicated to my mother
Joyce Catherine Kingdon

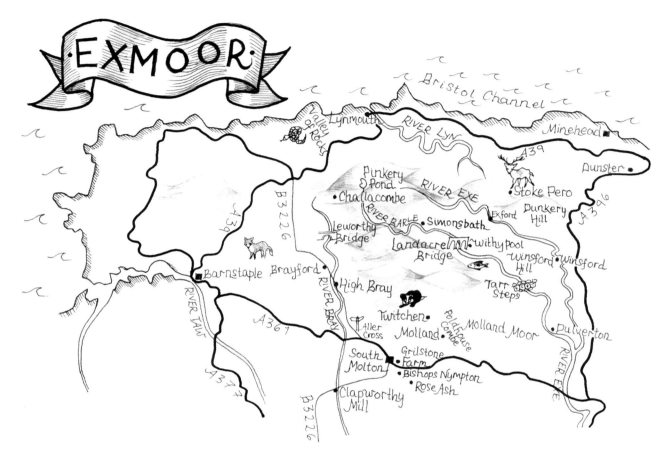

·EXMOOR·

Bristol Channel

Lynmouth
Valley of Rocks
RIVER LYN
Minehead
A39
Dunster
Pinkery Pond
RIVER EXE
Stoke Pero
Challacombe
Exford
Dunkery Hill
RIVER BARLE
Simonsbath
A396
Leworthy Bridge
Landacre Bridge
Withy pool
Winsford Hill
Winsford
B3226
Tarr Steps
Dulverton
Barnstaple
Brayford
High Bray
Twitchen
Poltimore Combe
Molland Moor
A39
RIVER BRAY
Aller Cross
Molland
A361
RIVER TAW
South Molton
Grilstone Farm
Bishops Nympton
Rose Ash
RIVER EXE
A377
Clapworthy Mill
B3226

Indi Davies

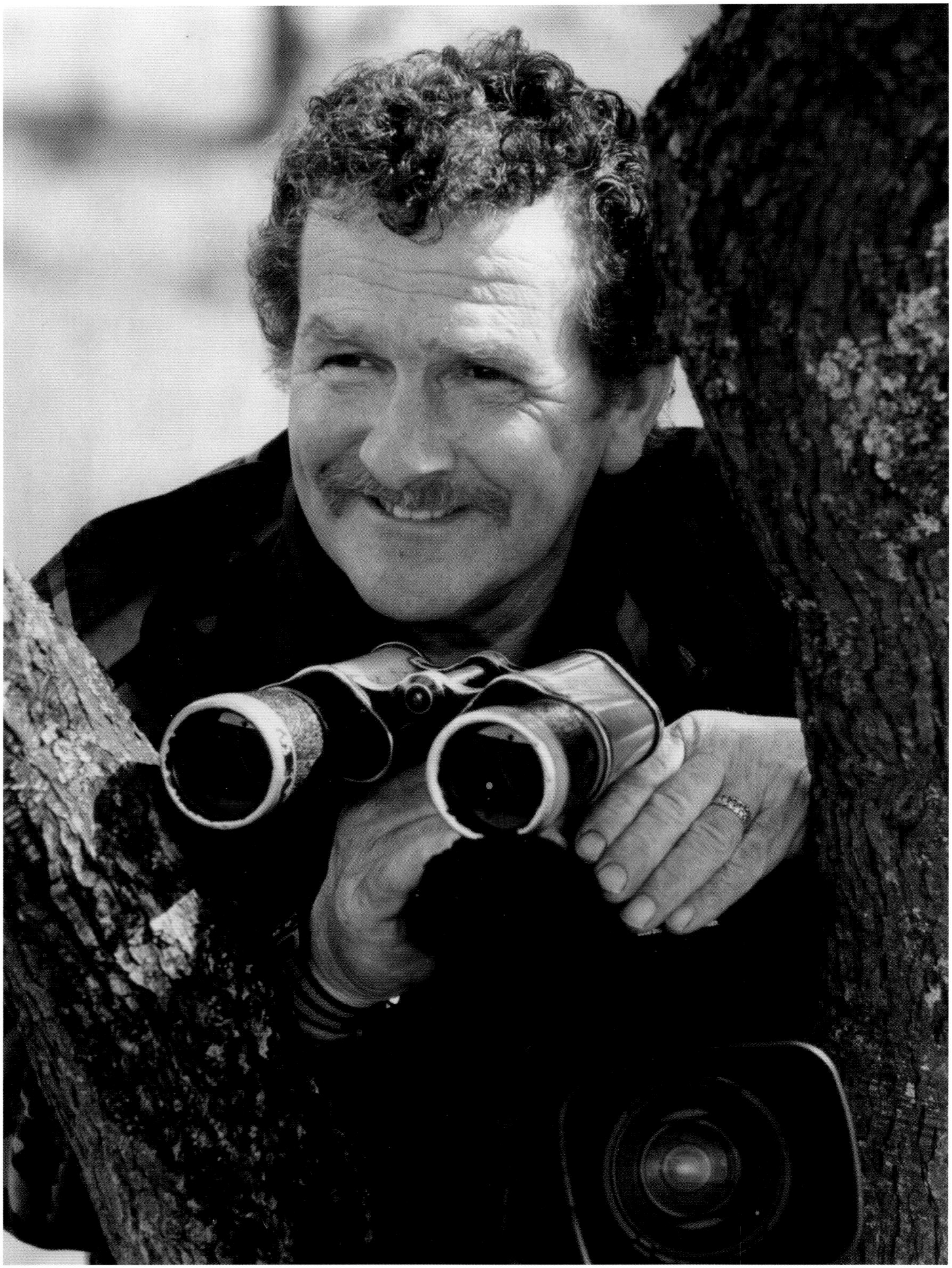
FREEMANS PRESS AGENCY

EARLY DAYS

It's 8.15 on a Sunday morning and the last 48 hours have been warm. I know this is a good time to film the stags; so I gather my gear and leave for the moor.

At Simonsbath last night there were 27 stags, so when I've picked up my friend John we head out that way. Sure enough, at Emmets Grange we see the deer through our field glasses, about a mile and a half away. We drive three miles around until we come up behind them, with the wind towards us, and then we park and walk across the open common. I leave John by a tree in a beech hedge, standing on the bank with a camera – he's hoping to get some shots of me with the deer – while I go down into a goyle, a steep valley, walk along the side of the river at the bottom, and then climb up the steep slope on the other side.

At the top I start to crawl on my hands and knees. This is wild country, and there are no paths. I keep going for about a quarter of a mile, feeling the water soaking through my clothes as I crawl through stands of rushes and marsh, taking care to keep the wind blowing towards me, away from the deer, and keeping the camera dry. I know I'm very close now. So making sure the wind's still towards me, I stop moving, look up through the rushes, and wait.

For 20 minutes nothing happens. Then suddenly a deer gets up, stretches and shakes itself. It's less than 20 yards away.

On the left-hand side of me there's a single deer, a pricket – a two-year-old with straight antlers – and it spots me. There's only one thing to do when this happens: you stay still, and outstare the stag.

I look straight at him. He looks at me, and then suddenly he moves to my right. Another stag gets up – it's just as though the first one told him about me – and looks my way. The game's up. So I take the lens cap off the camera, and very slowly get up on one knee.

Now that I'm a bit higher I can see that there are 17 of them, all stags, and two very close. With 34 eyes against my two, of course they've seen me now. Stags are very nervous, but I know that if you keep dead still there's a chance they'll lie down again.

It doesn't happen this time. They're getting up, and I know that in a moment they'll be gone. So I zoom back a bit and take five still shots, then a few seconds' filming with the video camera, and then they're trotting away. Four hours' work for a few seconds' film. It's normal; and it's worth it.

For more than 20 years I've filmed wildlife on Exmoor, the place where I was born. When I was young I was the biggest rogue in town, but as I've got older, and I've got to know the animals better, I've become softer and more patient. I've found that if you go to where the wild creatures live, onto the moor or into the woods, and wait for them there, you don't have to go looking for them – they'll come out to meet you. And that's when you'll really begin to understand their secret ways.

In my time I've been a farm worker, a quarry man, a lumberjack and a poacher. Apart from two years' National Service in the Army regimental police in Hong Kong, I've always lived on Exmoor. I can't imagine anywhere prettier. The very high ground is all empty moorland pasture, bracken and heather, with bogs that can trap you if you don't know where to go, and standing water reflecting the sky. In the spring of the year, when the flowers burst out and cubs are born, everything starts to move; in summer the moor's purple with heather, and yellow with gorse, and full of birdsong. Autumn brings the roaring of stags in rut to the woods and coombes, where the leaves are turning rusty gold in the cold mornings. That's when we have village parties and whist drives, and settle down for the long cold winter ahead, when the moor's brown and bare, with the wild ponies grazing on thorny gorse and dry bracken, and the salmon running up the rivers to the spawning beds.

I've been a gravedigger for 50 years, on and off, ever since my dad first took me out when I was 12. He was the gravedigger for the parish where I was born, and I helped him a lot. I've always liked churchyards. 'Come on, give me a hand, boy,' he'd say; and off we'd go, out into the dark night, with just a paraffin Tilley lantern for light. I was scared the first time I saw some bones and a skull come up on the fork. But the dead won't hurt you, that's what I say.

High Bray, where I was born

I got a fright once, though, when I went out with Uncle Derek to help dig a grave at High Bray cemetery. We'd been working together for a while, by the light of one Tilley lantern hung on a stick, when he decided to go for a cup of tea. 'Stay here, Johnny,' he said, and went off down the path, leaving me all alone. I worked on, and I was three parts down inside the grave when suddenly I heard a weird wailing noise.

My birthplace at High Bray, and the village pump

'What the hell's that?' I thought. I was so frightened that I hid in the grave at first. When I finally looked out over the edge I saw a strange white thing coming towards me through the gravestones.

I've never been so terrified. I jumped out of the grave, and ran out of that cemetery so fast that I didn't stop till I was home. It was only later that I found out it was Uncle Tony Moule dressed up in a white sheet, playing a game to scare me.

We lived in a cottage in High Bray, a small North Devon village with an old church, 10 miles from Barnstaple on the southern edge of the high moor. There was no electricity, and for a toilet we used a bucket in an old stone shed a little way from the house. Because I was the only boy in the family, when the bucket got full it was my job to empty it into a pit that dad and I dug in the garden, covering it over with earth. I hated doing it, and often used to sneak into the neighbours' shed and use their bucket so as to keep ours emptier for a bit longer. But my dad made sure we got good crops of vegetables from the places where we dug it all in.

My first pets were four tame black-and-white mice in a box, which Uncle Bert from Barnstaple brought me. They soon had babies; and with five or six babies at a time, I wasn't very long before I had 70 or 80 of them. They used to go up my sleeves and down my trouser legs, and crawl all over my body, and I made them little wheels and ladders to play on. My mum wasn't too pleased, but she didn't complain. She's a mum in a million. She had a very hard life with the six of us, but I never remember her interfering or shouting. Although dad's passed on now, we're all still very close to our mother, and even now we all live within 15 miles of each other.

My mum loved all wildlife, and she taught me to love animals too. As a boy I used to spend hours watching snails race. I'd collect them in culvert places, under stones or in walls, put them on a flat board with a line across it, and then see which one came to the top first.

I reared other creatures as well. Once I found two baby tawny owls on the ground. They had fallen out of their nest, so I took them home and reared them up on mice which I caught in my mother's larder. It was easy: all I had to do was set a trap last thing at night, baited with a bit of cheese, and in the morning I'd be guaranteed a mouse to feed to my owls. I did it for weeks and weeks, until they grew up and I let them go. But even after they were free, my owls would often fly up to the window late at night and tap the glass with a little scritching sound.

At night we went to bed carrying a candlestick, and we had a paraffin lamp for light downstairs. We fetched our water from a pump built over a well 100 yards away in the village square, which my great-grandfather had dug years before. We used to go to the pump carrying steel galvanised buckets, fill them with water for drinking, and bring them back to the larder, which was a small room off the main room downstairs. Every Friday night was bath night, and summer and winter we'd wait in turn to use the galvanised tin bath in front of the fire, filled with water brought from the buckets and heated on the stove.

I was brought up very poor. With so many children in the family, it was a case of one of this and one of that – we didn't have two of anything. As a young boy I used to poach fish, and I'd follow the rabbit man in the evening, watch where he set the gintraps, and beat him to them in the morning to take the rabbit, leaving a bit of paw in the trap to make it look as though it had got away. What I brought back from the traps often became our Sunday dinner.

We killed for the pot. We had to – with mum and dad, five girls and me in the family, life in the countryside was hard, and you did what you could to survive. My dad was a very tough man, who worked in Notts Quarries for 50 years setting explosives, and grew prizewinning vegetables and fruit in his garden. He believed in hard work. 'If you miss the morning, boy, you've missed the day,' he always told me. When we were little we used to go stealing his blackcurrants and gooseberries – goosegogs, we called them – which were big and juicy in your hand. We hid in the bushes and ate them raw, straight from the bush, as they came.

We'd find food outdoors wherever we could. In those days Whitefield Common was a moor – it's been reclaimed now for pasture and farm crops – and gangs of us used to go up there, or onto Molland Moor, and pick whortleberries, staining our hands and mouths and bringing back enough for whortleberry and apple pies, or to sell to the shops. Dad and Uncle Bert invented what they called a wort-picker to do the job better. It was a box-shaped shovel with stiff wire prongs on the front, and with it dad could pick pounds and pounds of worts at one go, and sell them to John Brooks's shop in South Molton, our local market town. When we were picking, his bucket always filled up much quicker than mine, though my berries were riper than his. At blackberry time we picked blackberries, and that was the time for blackberry pies. Later in the season came the sloes, to make into sloe gin for the gentry to drink at the autumn pheasant shoots.

We didn't have many toys. When I was three years old, my mum once gave me a tin of nails and staples to play with for a rattle. I sat down on the doorstep in

My dad winning the garden show outright

the sunshine with them, and knowing me, I opened the tin up and started putting them in my mouth. The next thing was, mum heard me crying. She came out to see what the matter was.

'What've you done, boy? What've you done?' she cried.

'I've ate a nail, Mother,' I wept.

It took 48 hours to go straight through me, and when it came out it turned out to be a big staple, an inch and a quarter long, with two sharp points. Luckily it must have gone down U first. I've still got that staple today, to remind me of my good luck right at the beginning of my life.

In my youth days I was a wild man. I always seemed to be in trouble, though at school they did their best to teach me the right way of doing things. Whenever I swore, the teacher made me wash my mouth out with soap. It didn't make a lot of difference to me, though – I just carried on swearing. That's the way I was.

If I swore at home dad would give me a clip round the ear. He didn't like bad language, because all our family believed in the Church. High Bray was a very religious place, and we were strong in belief. I used to go to church and Sunday school every week, and I sang in the church choir too, all dressed up in a long gown and a frilly collar. Often we couldn't ring the bells because of the jackdaws' nests. They'd build in the windows, and then they'd come in and build in the church tower under the bells as well. Jackdaws like to stay together, and they build big, untidy nests of sticks. We'd clear the sticks away every so often, and put wire across the windows to keep them out. But they'd find their way in again, just the same.

I was a natural left-hander, but at school the teacher tied my left hand behind my back to make me write with my right hand. My sister Julie used to sneak up behind the chair and try and untie the rope for me.

I was poor at most things at school. But I liked girls, and I was always chasing them. When I was 11 years old I once chased Julie Mayne right into a store cupboard in a corner of the playground. It was only when I closed the door that I found it was a self-locking system. We were in serious trouble: we couldn't get out, the teachers couldn't find a key to get in, and there we were, locked in together. I got six of the best with the cane that time. It didn't half hurt, but I thought it was worth it.

Things got no better when I got to the secondary modern school. I remember

Left to right: my sister Susan, me, my sister Julie, 1949

Brayford village: using my box Brownie camera, second from the right

how Mr Brown used to teach us agriculture and gardening outside in the fields.

'Hey, Johnny, get up in that hedge and pick me that stick,' he said to me once. 'That one there. Now come down here, boy.' Down I came, carrying the stick. 'Bend over now,' said Mr Brown; and he gave me six of the best for swearing. Even the woodwork teacher once threw a mallet at me for bad language. Afterwards he was very sorry, because he injured me: but he still didn't manage to cure me of my bad ways.

There was only one thing I was ever good at, and that was art. Nearly every summer I used to come first in class, and when someone gave me an old box Brownie camera I used to go round the village taking pictures of horses and cows and sheep. I used to like drawing the animals that I could see.

Although school was often frustrating, it didn't bother me too much, partly because I often used to miss it anyway. There were so many other exciting things to do. In winter, if it snowed, we'd play in the fields; in summer we would all go to the River Bray that ran through the village, and build a dam to make the water deeper for swimming. We spent many a summer day in the cool water, with the sun on our backs and all the moor above us.

The river had its secrets. I learnt very young how to tickle trout, one of my favourite things to eat. You get into the water, find where the trout is hiding under a stone, then very gently you put your fingers underneath it, feel where it is, and play with it a bit. As you play with the trout you corner it, and then you catch hold of it. I was always a sleepwalker – I did it so much that my parents tied the windows with a bootlace, for fear I'd fall out – and one night my father came in and found me on my knees with my hands under the pillow, tickling trout in a dream.

My friend Fred was a star trout-tickler. One Sunday we started at Brayford bridge and got all the way to Leworthy bridge near Ovis Farm. In that stretch of four or five miles we tickled everything in the river. We caught 87 trout and a young salmon that day.

Looking down the Barle valley towards Highnam Farm

I liked going fishing with Fred. Once we had seven good trout hanging up already on a forked stick cut from a hedge, when suddenly a fisherman appeared carrying a rod and line. He wasn't pleased to see us poaching.

'What do you think you're doing?' he said.

'Catching trout,' we answered, cool as anything.

'Do you know you're poaching? I've bought fishing rights on this stretch of river,' he said. You could tell he was getting angry.

'Well, where does your fishing ground start, sir?' I asked. I thought I'd be kind to him.

'Down river, from the bridge,' he pointed, 'and it goes upward from there.'

'All right, fair's fair,' I said. 'If you're fishing here, we'll start fishing down below the bridge.' So off we went with our fish, and we started again below the bridge. We knew we were being cheeky; but we were boys, and mad for the river.

Sometimes there was more serious poaching to do. My dad always said that a fish from the sea is anybody's, and in the evening time, once it was too dark for gardening, he often used to leave my mum and sisters at home and take me out looking for the salmon that came in from the sea to spawn where the Exmoor rivers rose. In 1952, the year of the great floods which washed away half of Lynmouth, when I was 14 years old, someone organised a big poaching night. My dad carried the light, three Tilley mantles inside a big lantern; and I went along to help carry the fish back.

It was very dark when we left the house to go from High Bray to Brayford to pick up the other men down at the bottom of the hill. We seemed to light up all of the village with our lantern as we walked out across the fields. I thought we'd get caught; but dad didn't care. He was a real hard man, and took us up the river as though we owned the place.

We spent until around midnight catching salmon, and then bagged them all up and turned for home. It was pouring with rain and very dark as we came to a bank where we knew there was a gap in the hedge, and I was just climbing through into the field, when all of a sudden there was a bright light in my face and men were coming at us from all directions carrying big sticks. It was the water bailiffs, and we were cornered. I was terrified. I dropped to my hands and knees like a rabbit, wriggled between their legs, and ran like hell.

The floods had washed down a big moot – an old tree-stump – into the middle of the field, and when I reached it I crouched down behind it and looked back. The bailiffs were looking for me with a large searchlight, and I could see my dad fighting. I watched him disappear over the barbed wire into the river with the other man, and when the light passed I took another run. I thought it best not to go home at all, so I made for Mr White's house in Brayford instead.

Mr White was a nice gentleman, with a big family of boys and girls. They were all fast asleep in bed when I turned up on his doorstep at dead of night, dripping wet and out of breath.

'I've runned away from the bailiffs, Mr White, what shall I do?' I said when he opened the door to my banging. He peered at me out of the dark house by the dim light of a candle.

'You'd better get up to bed with the boys,' he said, opening the door wide and taking me in.

That night I couldn't settle. The White boys slept in three separate beds, and I sleepwalked from one bed to the other all night, until in the end I'd slept in all three – a bit like Goldilocks and the Three Bears, but much wetter. When it started getting light, at 6 o'clock, they woke me and sent me home safely. I found when I got there that dad had got away, too, though they caught up with him later and he had to pay a £20 fine. The local paper carried the story, and to this day I remember the headline: 'Boy Disappears in Darkness'. That was me, giving the water bailiffs the slip; and it was the beginning of my real poaching days.

In those days we hadn't heard about looking after

North Exmoor coast, looking towards Ringer's Peak

wildlife. Birds and animals were an everyday part of our lives, and we didn't worry about them. The wildest and biggest, most beautiful creatures on the moor were the red deer, and hunting the stags was part of tradition. This is the way we were brought up, and when I was young we didn't know any different. The hunt was one of our favourite games. Because I was the ringleader the other village children always picked me as the stag, and all the rest were the hounds. They'd give me half an hour and then start the chase.

Once when we were playing at hunting I took off from near the bridge at Brayford and ran up the river through the woods to Little Bray. At Broomhill Villas, on the edge of the village, I could hear the others not far behind; so I climbed up onto the top of some garages and started jumping from roof to roof. It was all going well until I jumped onto a roof made of asbestos, went straight through it and landed on top of an Austin 7 car.

The noise brought the others out, but before we could get away we saw people hurrying down from a distance from the houses above. I didn't know whose garage roof I'd broken until I heard Mr Dinnage shouting.

'Little sods! What've you done now? You'll pay for this, Johnny Kingdom! You'll pay for this!' he yelled. He hadn't seen the marks on the Austin 7 car yet. Although I was stuck in the garage, panic got me up through the roof again and I ran for it. I got into real trouble that time.

We had a lot of freedom in our childhood. On fine days we'd go out to the high cliffs along the Exmoor coast, where the blue Bristol Channel stretched out far below, and look for seagull eggs, which we sold to the hotels for a penny each. We walked miles after jackdaws' eggs, too, until one Sunday I was with my mates David and Brian when we came across an empty house that hadn't been lived in for quite a long time. No-one was about, so we decided to break a window, climb inside and take the eggs from the jackdaws' nest we could see was in the chimney. We didn't think we were harming anyone, and we wanted the eggs badly.

Jackdaws build with sticks, but their nests are beautifully tidy inside, lined with sheep's wool, and their eggs are blue with black spots, and very pretty. We thought we had a good chance when we saw that the fireplace was full of sticks that had fallen down from the nest above. But we couldn't reach the nest itself; so David decided to climb up and get it. He stripped all his clothes off, got into the fireplace and wriggled up inside the chimney, until all we could see were the tips of his toes dangling down. And then he got stuck.

What a fool. He couldn't move, neither up nor down, no matter how hard he tried. We were getting worried, and in the end we could only think of one way out. We took up a pickaxe that was lying in the corner, and broke through the stones of the chimney-breast itself. Sure enough, we got David out; but we'd wrecked the whole wall doing it.

More to the point, we still hadn't got our eggs. Then I thought of the drainpipe outside, where there was another big nest on top of the funnel. We went out, and I began to climb. I was nearly at the roof when the brackets came out of the wall, the whole drainpipe came down, and I fell onto the ground straight onto my belly. It was a long drop, but I was none the worse for it, though really I was a very lucky lad to be alive.

We went home covered in soot, and said nothing. But we'd been seen, and the next morning a policeman came to school looking for us. Once again I was in trouble. He cautioned us for the damage we'd done, but even worse from our point of view was the hiding we all got from our parents.

After I left school I worked for two years on a farm. Mr Tucker, the boss, was kind to me, and set me to work with Mr Erne Johns, who showed me how to cut grass and hoe mangels and swedes. In those days farming was a really hard battle, and every acre had to be worked by hand. We used carthorses to plough and chain-harrow the ground ready for sowing, and it was my job to look after them. They were huge animals, and very strong.

One Sunday afternoon near the rectory of High Bray, we decided to go for a horse ride. So Jim Venn brought his big carthorse round to the top of a steep cleeve, and eight of us got onto it, like Uncle Tom Cobley and all, one behind the other. When we were all up Jim smacked the horse's backside, and it took off like a rocket down the slope, faster and faster as the field got steeper. It wasn't long before we started falling off, left, right and all ways. In the end there was only little Ruth Madox left, hanging on to the horse's mane for dear life while it galloped down the field. We really thought she might be hurt. But that maid stayed on the horse's back all the way down the hill.

At home my dad kept us all in order, but we bent the rules whenever we could. In the evening times, after work, I used to wait for my older sister Shirley to come in. She was a tomgirl, and she was often out courting very late. She'd sneak into the house by getting up onto the big steel water drum outside,

Courting days: Julie and me, aged 16 and 19

catching hold of the guttering and climbing up over the roof and into the window. One night my sister Julie, who shared a bed with her, got annoyed at being woken up. 'Dad, Shirley's come in!' she shouted. She knew that he'd leather Shirley with a belt buckle for being so late. And he did; but unluckily for Julie, when he came into the dark bedroom, belt in hand, it was her, not Shirley, who he leathered by mistake. That was the last time she told tales.

After two years I left the farm and went to work at Notts Quarries with my dad and Uncle Tony, ripping out stones with an iron bar. In the evenings dad trained me to box. Uncle Arthur gave me some boxing gloves, and I got quite good at it, until one night I bettered my dad and smacked him one. He got really mad, and came at me like a rocket. It was lucky I stepped out of the way; he was a good boxer, and if he'd hit me he would have taken my head right off my shoulders. Instead he passed me so fast that his fist went straight through the cupboard door behind me, right in amongst the dishes, with such a noise that my mother woke up and wondered what the hell was going on down in the kitchen at 11 o'clock at night. We had a job getting dad's hand out of the cupboard door, it was wedged in so tight. The crack in the door was there for many years afterwards.

I first met my wife, Julie, when I was 17 and she was 13, and not long afterwards I saw her again at the South Molton carnival, where she was crown-bearer for the Carnival Queen. After the carnival I went to the pub and drank so much cider that when I came out I fell down and cut my nose. But I still managed to get to the carnival dance at the Assembly Rooms that night.

I met Julie there and sat down beside her. But her brother Terry was angry, and took her aside. 'I don't want to see you going with that man again,' he warned her. You could see his point. When I came out of the Assembly Rooms that night I was so drunk that I tumbled all the way down the 25 steps to the pavement below. Cider can get to you sometimes.

I've always been a cider man. The cider we drank was mostly from Clapworthy Mill on the Exeter road; but most of the farmers around the moor made their own as well. Real rough cider should be yellow, and cloudy, and it should give you a good kick. I can't understand anyone wanting to take drugs. Have a pint of farm-brewed cider, that'll make you go – and it'll do you good, too.

When Julie was 16 I took her home to High Bray for the first time. It was soon after we'd had electric light installed in the house, and I wanted to show it off. So after we'd been sitting on the couch together for an hour or two, and the room was getting very dark, I told her to go and put the light on. As she crossed the room I heard a snickling, snackling noise. Of course, I knew what it was, because I lived there; but when she put the light on she had the fright of her life, and ran back onto the couch fast. The floor was crawling with black beetles.

We were used to them. They crept out every night when it was dark, and my mum always used to put cucumber skins down to poison them. It got rid of them for a while, but they always came back. There were crickets in the walls, too; you

In the Regimental police, Hong Kong, 1958

could often hear them chirruping. The house was owned by Mr Thorne from the village of Ben Twitchen, a real old-timer in a brown trilby hat with a fag hanging out of his mouth, who came every Friday to collect the rent and mark us off in his little rent-book. They were very old cottages, and in the end the council bought them and modernised them. But that wasn't until much later.

When I was 19 I was called up for National Service. Most of the lads went off to work on farms instead, to avoid having to serve. But I looked at it differently. The furthest I'd been was Barnstaple, 10 miles away, and I wanted to prove myself and see something different; so I thought I'd take my chance, and I volunteered for Hong Kong, ten thousand miles away.

I'd never seen anything like the Army. You had to be a very fit person to be accepted. I passed the medical test, and I was very, very keen, and tried my best. But it didn't matter what you did, they always found fault with you. I used to do my kit just right, ten inches across – I measured it with a ruler – and yet they'd still come in, pull it all on the ground and give the order: 'Do it again, Kingdom!' You couldn't swear at them, or you'd be put inside; so you had to do it again, and again, until it was perfect. Army life was a very hard thing, and in those early days I was a worried man. But in the end it did me a favour, because it put me in my place. At home in High Bray I thought I was king. But it took the Army to make a man of me.

I still broke the rules sometimes, though. In Hong Kong I had 22 tattoos done, in the Chinese tattoo workshops on the Nathan Road in Kowloon, which was strictly forbidden. One of the pictures I love best is on my chest. It shows Jesus on the cross with the angels, and it means that I hope the Lord helps me on my way always, because I do believe in Him. It's a detailed picture, and took a long time to do. They didn't use anaesthetic in the Chinese workshops of Hong Kong. It took some strong drink, beer mixed with spirits, to get through that tattooing.

While I was in the Army I kept a picture of Julie with me on my dresser. Though Hong Kong was exciting, I couldn't wait to get back to Exmoor again. I've always loved my own country.

The day I came home I was the only person to step down off the train at South Molton into the warm sunshine. I didn't arrive with much: just one case, tied round with a big rope where it had broken on the sea crossing. It was strange to be back home.

Walking up North Street in South Molton, the Barnstaple Inn caught my eye. There'd been no pubs in Hong Kong, and I was feeling very dry, so of course I went straight inside. That very day I hit the cider again, and I got so drunk that Billy Yeo had to come to the pub and fetch me home to face my mother.

Mum was so pleased to see me, she didn't care about the cider. She just burst into tears, and so did I. It had been a long 19 months for her, waiting for her lad who had never been away from home before.

As soon as I got back Julie was ringing up, and it wasn't long before I met her mum and dad. Julie lived in a cottage at Grilstone Farm, where her father was the farm bailiff. Her parents weren't too pleased about me at first, knowing my reputation as a hard drinker and poacher with wild ways. But they came to accept me, and in the end we got on very well.

For nights on end I'd borrow my sister Shirley's old bike – I couldn't afford one of my own – and cycle the 13 miles to Grilstone Farm to see Julie. I thought the world of her. I didn't have the money for lights, and I always cycled without.

One evening as I was cycling back in the dark along the turnpike road past Bray Valley Quarries, where I worked, I saw a car parked ahead of me with the sidelights on. I thought of the police, and started pedalling hard. But as I came alongside the car, a hand came out and caught me by the collar, holding me so stiff in the air that I was lifted straight out of my seat, and the bike just carried on without me. 'Where do you think you're going, boy?' said PC Walters sternly. I was summonsed after that, and told to appear in court. My mother stepped in and wrote a letter explaining that I'd just come out of the Forces, and in the end all I had to pay was a ten-shilling fine. Though I've done so much poaching in my time, the only fine I've ever had was for riding a bike without any lights.

After I left the Army my poaching days were still in me, and I used to go out at weekends and take rabbits, salmon, even the odd deer. I got a kick out of it. No-one ever caught me, though I often gave the bailiffs a good chase. Once I was coming down from High Bray with my young cousin Steve, to go fishing in the river. But no sooner had we climbed over a gate than Mr Wilmot, the bailiff, came over the other side and we had to run for it. I was a very fit boy, but Steve wasn't so quick. 'Steve! Get in there,' I said, and pushed him into some thick brambles. Mr Wilmot ran right past us and never found us, poor man. I don't do these things now – I'm older and wiser. But in those days it was a challenge.

Julie and I married a year later, at Bishop's Nympton Church, where my two youngest sisters Rosie and Thelma were bridesmaids; and we went to live in Bishop's Nympton, where our two sons Stuart and Craig were born and where we still live today.

When word spread that I was moving there, some people in Bishop's Nympton were a bit worried. They knew I was a poacher, and George, another well-known poaching man and a great mate of mine, lived there too. Two poachers getting together would make things more awkward for the farmers, who liked to take a bit of game themselves, though they'd never have admitted it.

Working at Notts Quarries: Uncle Harry second from left, me on the right

I've seen a farmer put the fender down on the millstream at Brayford, stop the water for a few minutes and stab the trapped salmon with a pitchfork – a dungpick, as we call it. A farmer I knew years ago used to walk over the stone Brayford bridge quite regularly with a West of England sack over his shoulder, and the blood dripping out of it onto the road from the freshly killed salmon inside. He was a nice chap, but he was just like the rest of us – he loved a bit of salmon. He was one of the people who used to tell me to leave the salmon alone.

Brayford being such a religious place, with no pubs, I used to go drinking with Uncle Harry and Uncle Tony at the Poldimore Arms, three miles out of the village up a steep hill towards Simonsbath. I'd bought a James 197 motorbike by now, and I used to get so drunk it was a trouble to get myself home sometimes. We hadn't even heard of drink-driving in those days, and more than once we ended up in the ditch.

Harry used to drive an old Austin 7 box car, and one evening when we came out of the pub I got on my bike and drove round and round him, for a laugh. It terrified him, and he refused to drive home in front of me in case I crashed into him. So I took off before them down Beer Hill, and once I was out of sight I decided to have a bit of a joke. I parked the bike up at the right-hand side of the road and twisted the light so that it was pointing up into the trees, as though I'd had an accident. Then I went down the road and lay in the gutter; but I was too drunk to notice that I'd left my leg hanging out in the road.

Down came the car, and of course they saw the bike and the light in the trees straight away. Harry tried to pull over to one side, when all of a sudden they heard a bang and felt the car bump. They'd driven right over my leg.

'Oh no, we've killed the bugger!' Tony shouted out as they came to a stop 25 yards down the road. Uncle Harry stayed in the car, cowering, as Tony came running back to where I was. By the time he reached me I'd got on my feet and was back on the motorbike again.

'You silly sods, didn't you see me there?' I shouted. 'You could've killed me.' I thought it was funny, but it took a while for Harry to see the joke. Still, there was no harm done, though I went to work the next morning with the print of an Austin 7 tyre on the inside of my leg.

It was a real accident that turned me into a film-maker, though. After 11 years at the quarry I'd become a lumberjack, doing heavy and quite dangerous work with explosives as well as felling big trees. Normally I worked with Robin Dyer, who was my best mate in those days. One day, though, he was away and I was on my own, driving a 4-wheel-drive tractor with a winch and chains attached to the back for hauling timber. As I was reversing, looking back over my right shoulder, one of the chains broke. The steel bar of the hydraulic arm sprang back through the back of the tractor cab and smashed right into my face just below my eye.

For a while I lay unconscious on the floor of the cab. When I came round I was lying in a pool of blood by the side of my truck, with my big lurcher dog, Sandy, licking my face. It was badly fractured in four places, and I'd dislocated my jaw. By rights I should have died.

I'll never know how I drove home. Halfway there I pulled into a layby and sat wondering, half-delirious. I thought that someone had given me a hiding, but I couldn't remember why. My wife got the shock of her life when she saw me walk in through the door that day.

After several operations to put my face right I had 22 weeks off work, and that was when I lost my nerve completely. I went on Valium tablets to cope with the nightmares. I was afraid to go back to the lumberjacking, it seemed so dangerous. Everything was gone, and I didn't know what to do next.

It was about this time that people were beginning to buy the first video cameras. My mate Roger Gregory from South Molton had one, and one day I borrowed it from him, and drove up to the moors.

It lifted me up to be back after I'd been away for so long, and pulled down so low. Exmoor's in my blood, and being on the high, wild ground, with the skylarks singing over the purple heather and the fresh wind in my face, was like coming back into the world again.

I had a notion that I'd try to film some deer. It didn't take long to find a group of hinds, near Zeal Farm, not far from Anstey Common. So I pulled over, carefully got out of the truck and walked towards them. The deer stayed within

YORKSHIRE TELEVISION

This is how my film-making began

view, and I even got a few clear shots. I thought I'd got on quite well. It was only when I played the film back later, at home, and saw nothing but ground, earth, stones, water and grass, that I understood I'd left the camera running the whole time.

But I had to go back. I had to do it again. I've always been a highly strung person, and filming the animals and birds and the moor I loved made me feel different, calmed me down. The moments on the moor were mine, and I discovered an enjoyment I'd never known. I got my own camera, a Panasonic MS1 Super VHS at first, later a Hi-8 and then finally a DV Cannon XL1S. I started going up onto the moors regularly, filming rabbits and birds, deer and foxes, badgers and squirrels. I'd known them well in my poaching years. But it wasn't until I began to watch them properly that Exmoor came to life for me in a new way.

SPRING

Exmoor is small for a National Park. Measuring only 265 square miles, it lies partly in West Somerset and partly in North Devon. It's a world of its own, stretching out from the rocky cliffs of the cold Bristol Channel, across the moor, to the green fertile fields of farmland in the south. Famous rivers run through it, the Barle, the Exe, rising in small waters on the high, lonely ground where the salmon runs and the otter goes its secret ways.

The rivers flow down into the coombes and valleys, where thick covers of oak grow twisted and low, following the shelter of the hillsides. This is the home of the red deer and the shy, small roe deer, the woodpeckers and badgers, the squirrels and foxes, and when you walk there you hear the bright song of birds. There are old stone-built bridges, lanes and high beech-topped hedgerows, old paths and secret byways.

Exmoor ponies at Withypool Common

Rainbow over Exmoor

Villages lie all around the moor, as they have for hundreds of years, with daffodil-scattered grass verges, pubs, farms and cottages, and stone churches with their cemeteries. I've dug many a grave there over the years, said goodbye to many a friend and relative as I've laid them to rest.

At Molland Church the primroses come out in their hundreds in the early spring, small pale flowers dotting the grass. The church is eight or nine hundred years old, so the primroses have had a long time to spread out there. Inside the church you've got a job to see the vicar, because the wooden pews are so high. That's how it was years ago in the house of prayer, and it's still the same today.

High above the villages, there's the wide open moor where the wild ponies eat the prickly gorse and the skylark sings. Though in the spring it still looks very bare, you'll often see a rainbow, sometimes two, at this time of year. They always say that there's a lump of gold at the end of the rainbow; but I haven't found it yet.

Our Exmoor winters are bleak and frosty, snowy on the high land and brown and bare below. But in the spring everything's on the move. Everything's happening, building, mating: the birds nest, the leaves come out, and life begins.

For me it's a good time of the year to film. In April there'll be the first sighting of the fox cubs, followed by the badger cubs. By the second week in June, with the thorn trees in leaf, the red deer calves are being born. The migrating birds come across to nest, the swallows, swifts and the spotted flycatcher. There's lots to see and you can never get it all.

The start of spring is cold, and sometimes it brings late snows which leave the cows in the fields very shivery. I talk to the animals when I see them so miserable. 'Hello, good morning, it's cold this morning,' I'll say, and they'll stare back at me. When people hear me talking like this, they think I'm mad; but that's just the way I am. The fat cows, the true beef cows of Exmoor, are the best beef you can have; but when it snows they hardly get a blade of grass, and they have to wait for the farmer to make it up to the hills and put a bale of hay in their rack.

SPRING

Primroses at Molland Church

Cows in snow near Sandy Way

Lambs' tails, the flower of the hazel tree

Flock of ewes and lambs near Molland Moor

On Exmoor we say that you'll see the lambs' tails on the hazelnut trees when the lambs are in the fields. In the winter life is slow; but when spring comes the farmers are busy from morning till dusk. If the weather's cold the ewes are kept in yards and sheds, and they feed on sheep cake; but if it's nice and mild the farmer will put them out to grass, putting cake out in troughs to fatten them and grow their lambs. As the lambs are born he paints a number on each one, along with its mother, so that he can tell which lambs and ewes belong together; and then no matter what the weather, he'll put them out in the fields, where he's been growing good grass for them all winter.

But all this time other creatures have been visiting the farmers' fields regularly, coming like a quiet guest to the table from the surrounding woods and valleys. Our red deer are impressive animals, and Exmoor is the only place in England where they still run wild. At the end of the winter they like nothing better than to eat the farmer's juicy young grass.

Up on Winsford Hill where the fieldfare flocks in the thorn trees, there's wild copse land and rough pasture. But a glimmer of sun will bring out the deer in the farmland below, where on a sunny day you might see big groups of hinds and yearlings, 20, 30 or 40 of them, sitting in a field enjoying the early warmth. From a distance they look relaxed, but if you approach they'll disappear instantly into some deep valley or wood. There is nothing tame about them.

Many farmers like the deer, but they worry a lot about the damage they do. Deer will nibble a whole field of swedes or carrots. Even if there's one bite taken out of a vegetable, the farmer can't sell it. As well as eating his crops, the stags and hinds will use three or four gaps in a farmer's hedge to get into a field, which they make wider as they go backwards and forwards; and mending hedges is expensive. From the farmer's point of view, they're doing damage all the time.

At the beginning of spring the deer still have their rough, shaggy winter coats, before they get the reddish summer coat that gives them their name. The hinds are pregnant at this time of year, ready to drop their calves in June; and the stags meet up with their old pals again. Last autumn they had vicious fights, during the rutting season; but now all that's forgotten and they're friendly. They'll form big herds, thirty or forty together, their antlers like moving tree branches as they run along the valleys and through the woods.

The reason the stags group together like this is that from early March until June they all shed their antlers. The biggest and oldest lose theirs first, around the second week in March; and the rest of the herd follows, all growing fresh antlers in the summer ready for the autumn rutting season. But getting antlers to drop can be tricky sometimes; so the stags help each other.

I've seen it happen. The animal feels an irritation around his horns, and he pushes them against a tree or on the ground. Like a wobbly tooth, the antlers get looser and looser, so that in the end the least little jerk can make them fall like a nut out of a shell. But a big antler can weigh six pounds or more, and when it snaps off and hits the ground it makes such a noise that it can frighten the whole herd. A lopsided head isn't easy to manage, and so the stags lock heads together and push each other's antlers off. They'll even stand on their hind legs to do it better.

Stalking along the river one day in late March, I once got within 15 paces of a stag trying to knock his antlers off by rubbing them on a tree. He was damaging the tree doing it, leaving bark lying in long strips on the ground. But he couldn't help it. It was in his nature. He just had to scratch his itching head.

Once the antlers are off you can see that the stags are relieved, and they relax and start nibbling the grass. They need the food: it takes only three or four days before their new antlers start to grow. These are just blackish bumps at first, then as they grow and spring turns to summer, they become soft and velvety; and next autumn's lethal weapons are on their way.

You can tell a lot about a deer by its antlers, including its age. The points normally grow in a certain order. A yearling has no antlers at all. A two-year-old, what we call a pricket, will have two short, straight horns. The third year, a stag grows his brow points, sticking straight out from his forehead; on the fourth, he

In spring the stags lose their antlers

The points on a stag's antler

Showing an antler to schoolboys, Poldhouse Combe cave

adds the next ones up – his bay points; in the fifth, he adds another level – his trey points. We call this framework the stag's 'rights'; and when he has them all he'll be five years old. For the following three years he'll grow his top points, one on each side per year. So a royal, or eight-year-old stag in good health has all his rights, that is, brow, bay and trey; and three points on top. If each antler is perfect, he'll have twelve points in all.

Deer kept on a deer farm will grow a head like this within three years, because they eat rich food and calf cake; but in the wild it generally takes eight years. These are the antlers that everyone's after, the perfect stag's glory. But as a stag gets older his antlers begin to wear out, and eventually they'll become clumpy, with no points, and start growing in a cup formation. A stag like this should be culled, because he's no good to the herd.

On Exmoor we know a stag by his antlers, and many people like to pick them up. The deer soon forgets his discarded antlers: I've watched a stag find one on the ground, sniff it and push it out of his way before moving on. Not so the human beings. For us they're a good trophy, something to display, sell or make things out of, and finding them is a big craze. People walk for miles looking for them every spring, often going out with torches in the early morning to be the first to pick up any that have fallen the night before. Staghorns are the symbol of Exmoor, and a fine pair of antlers can fetch good money.

People treasure them too, handing them down through generations of the same family. More than 60 years ago, when he was out shooting pigeons, my dad found a lovely pair, lying side by side under a beech tree. It happened only once in his whole life, and I've still got those antlers mounted on my wall today.

People have used staghorns as tools for thousands of years, and still today they're used for making candlesticks, whistles, hunting crops, letter knives – souvenirs for visitors and locals

All his rights and three a-top: the points on a royal stag

alike. Up at Hawkridge I know a man who has made a whole antler chair, with the horns all wound in and around the seat; and at Dulverton there's someone with a clever spaniel dog that's specially trained to pick them up. Staghorns hang on many pub walls on the moor, a reminder of the wilderness outside the door. There are staghorn shows on Exmoor, at Porlock, Quantock Hills and Tiverton, where alongside the gymkhana they'll judge the best antlers found that year from 30 or 40 entries, and award a cup, shield or rosette. I won the Porlock cup myself once, when I found a perfect pair through a real stroke of luck.

It was 10 April one year when a stag across a valley caught my eye, and I began watching him with field glasses. He was a fine animal, a royal stag with a perfect head, all his rights and three points on top, both sides. As I watched him lying on his own in a steep cleeve I thought, 'He's going to drop his antlers soon, for sure.' Not long afterwards I saw that he had only one left.

People often try and pick up one antler before the stag has dropped both. Usually all this does is frighten him into running away, carrying the other antler off with him. I sat tight. Stags can run many miles, and Exmoor's a big place.

Four days later my patience paid off. There he was, lying in the same spot with no antlers at all. As I hurried over to where he'd been, I wondered whether I'd be lucky. I could hardly believe it when I saw them lying there, two perfect antlers, crossed, on the ground. It was such a thrill to find them.

My cousin Terry Moule and his wife Rosemary have the finest collection of antlers in the South-West. They'll travel miles, following the deer, to pick up good sets, and Terry mounts them himself. I started Terry off, years ago when he used to ride on the back of my motorbike, and at Blackmoor Gate I found one

*Sunrise on Molland Moor
with Exmoor ponies*

antler with all its rights and two points on top. We hunted high and low for the other, and three days later Terry found it. 'I could do with the one you've got, Johnny,' he said; so I gave it to him, to pair them up. For him it was the beginning of a lifelong quest.

I don't have time to be looking for staghorns when I'm filming; though sometimes I'll come across odd ones anyway, on the earth or in the mud wallows where the deer roll to get rid of the ticks in their coats. It's strange to find them there, dead and abandoned, with just the points looking up out of the water, like a last memory of the winter that's past.

Up on the highest parts of the moor, the spring of the year brings the wild foals. You'd be very lucky to catch sight of an Exmoor foal being born. They're very small, shaky little things at first, and dainty-looking, though their mothers are hardy animals that take no harm in the high cold weather. The Exmoor pony is Britain's oldest breed of horse, and with only a few hundred left, it's scarcer than the giant panda. People sometimes ride them, but mostly they run wild on the moor. Unlike Dartmoor ponies, they're purebred, saved by the height and isolation of the land in centuries gone by, and carefully managed and maintained today by the farmers who own them and who take a few off the moor every year for sale. At this time of year they're losing their dull, shaggy winter coats and thick manes for their lovely, bright, gingery colours of summer.

This is the time when the hedges are being cast in the lower valleys as the first green buds begin to sprout. When I worked on farms years ago hedging was a tough job that you had to do by hand, using a staff and a hook, wearing a leather glove on your arm against the vicious thorns of the sloe bushes in the hedges. Nowadays it's often done by machine, which is less kind to the wildlife, but more efficient.

The cold weather doesn't last. When the hawthorn trees begin to bud, and the shoots come out and green up, you know that up on the moors there'll be blossom on the whortleberries, very small red flowers like currants. And as the sun climbs higher and the nights pull back, it's time to start looking for the badgers to come out.

Badgers have lived on Exmoor at least as long as people have; in fact, they were probably here first. They have their underground secrets, and like all our animals, they're shy and wary. You have to watch them for a long time to understand how clever and strong they are. They live in setts, networks of underground tunnels which they like to build at the edge of a piece of woodland, not too far from a farm. Their cubs are born in January, but they'll choose a warm spring evening when the light is fading, around the second week in April, to come out for the first time, when the bluebells are beginning to send up shoots and the celandines are in flower.

I never tire of it. Seeing the badger cubs emerge is one of the best moments of the filming year. You'll hear them squeaking and grunting underground for a while before they come out, as they begin to play and bite each other. It's fantastic to watch as the cubs come out from their hole, very small and wobbly; and then in May, as they get more sure, there's nothing better than seeing them play. I've learnt that you have to time it right, keep the wind blowing towards you and stay very quiet, or the mother badger will sense you're there. The cubs are excited and curious, but as each one comes out into the world she keeps her nose stretched out above it, scenting the air to make sure everything's safe.

I love filming the badgers, but you have to wait hours and hours sitting still and hidden to get a good shot. So about ten years ago I decided to build somewhere to sit. I chose a sett, and asked the farmer if I could put up a hide. It was up on a stand, open to the

A badger cautiously looks out of its hole to make sure everything is safe

Two badger cubs playing at night

A little badger cub, taking nuts out of a pipe

My badger playground

weather and not very strong: it used to rock crazily whenever the wind blew. But it gave me somewhere to stand with my camera while the badgers came out below and ate the treats I'd brought them.

I started by buying some big sacks of clean peanuts, which I knew badgers could eat safely. For the first two or three months I just left peanuts near the holes of the sett, so that the badgers got to like them. Then I hid them in little pits I'd dug, so that they'd have to try a bit harder and find them by scent. Julie made badger cakes next, of Sugar Puffs, fat, peanuts and honey, which kept them interested. By now I was filming them regularly, and I buried a square steel plate near the holes, connected to a microphone with a remote-control cable, so that I could record the sound of them snacking. I soon had enough footage to make a complete video film, which I began to edit on a small home edit suite.

Then the dairy herd of the farmer who owned the land got TB. The badgers came under suspicion and had to be destroyed, and I had to look for somewhere else.

Terry, a farmer I knew well, came to the rescue. 'Johnny, bring your hide to my land,' he said to me one day, 'I know you look after all the animals.' He let me have the use of three acres not far from South Molton, to look after the badgers and all the wildlife in and around the area. It was just what I needed.

The new hide was stronger and more comfortable, standing well off the ground, with a proper roof and windows, and with benches inside to sit down on. The badgers got a better deal too. First I put a few peanuts on the ground, and then some in a plastic pipe, to tempt them to stand on their hind legs. I said to myself, well, I wonder if they'll climb up a ladder? And I started to build a four-foot long ladder with a platform and a stool at the top. There I bored a hole for another pipe, and put nuts in that one too, with a ramp to get up to it. Badgers have very sensitive smell, but poor sight, so I poured honey onto the ramp to teach them the right way to go.

They were interested. These shy wild animals, which mostly come out in the evening to eat slugs and worms, beetles and the occasional small animal, took a great liking to the peanuts, and seemed not to mind following the ramps and reaching into the pipes. Badgers are clever and inquisitive, built like small English bears, with big, sharp claws, strong arms and good thick fur, and within 12 months they were happily walking up and down the ramps and walkways to get their peanuts. Then I began to think what else I could do.

I'd never forgotten my black-and-white mice of years before, with their ladders and wheels. The badger had walkways and ladders, I thought, so why not a wheel? I decided to give it a try.

The first badger wheel was quite small, only three feet around, with another pipe and a honey pot on top so that the badger had to stand up and put his nose in. A couple of months later my friend Gordon and I made a bigger version, and I started putting peanuts inside it so that the badgers would learn to turn it to get the peanuts out.

They completely ignored it, and I saw that I had to find some stronger attraction. So I tried honey.

It worked. Badgers love wild honey, and they're not worried by stings: I've seen a badger eat right through a wasps' nest, licking out every single grub and ignoring the angry wasps. They soon went round the walkways, found the wheel and learnt to stand on their hind legs to lick it. But a swarm of wild bees found it too, which meant no filming unless I wanted to be badly stung. I had no choice but to stay away until the badgers and the bees between them finished the honey.

Sow badger looking for peanuts

WESTERN DAILY PRESS

Once the bees had gone I started again with the peanuts, and waited patiently. It took 9 months before a badger turned the wheel; but once they'd got the hang of it I started getting such lovely shots that all the effort seemed worth it. I began selling the video I'd made of them, and many people rang up and said how much they enjoyed it. The hide became a place for watching badgers, and I used to take people there in small groups to watch for themselves. We saw many generations of cubs grow up over the seven years we were there.

I brought in an old pigs' trough for water so that they didn't have to go near the road to the river, and even made a very small wheel for the badger cubs to play with. A pub landlord let me have an old beer barrel, and I drilled holes in it, painted it green, and in less than a week a cub was turning it. In the end we even planted flowers, and a hedge to keep the wind off and hide us. But no matter how used to us the animals got, they would never come out if the wind was in the wrong direction and they scented us.

My new hide at Twitchen

SPRING

In 2001 a sad thing happened when foot and mouth disease hit Exmoor. The countryside was closed down and I couldn't get to the badger hide for nine months. When I got back I found that the land just below it had been sold, and the new owner didn't want anyone crossing his land. This was the only way in to the badger hide, so it meant that I could never go there again. It was a terrible shock to me.

A few days afterwards a kind farmer in Twitchen, Tony Thorne, gave me permission to build a hide by a sett on his land, where an oak wood met a steep field halfway down a valley. It was a help, after my big loss, to have somewhere to start again. With the help of my sons Stuart and Craig, Pete Webster, and a small gang of other friends, the new hide was finished six weeks later, and I could begin working with the wildlife. I started by feeding birds.

At first, in winter, there seemed to be no birdlife at the new hide at all, except for an owl, calling through the lonely wood. After a few weeks' feeding, though, and with the turning of the season into spring, things had changed. I'd seen blue tits, great tits – we call them tom tits – chaffinches, marsh tits, woodpeckers, coal tits, goldfinches, goldcrests, our smallest bird, bullfinches, long-tailed tits, and robins; and many of these birds came to feed every day. I'd hear the rattle of the nuthatch far away in the woods. Sometimes I'd see a fox sitting cleaning himself, or some hinds making their stately way through the wood. And there were lots of squirrels.

For weeks on end that spring I'd go to the hide, only to find the walls of the top and bottom rooms of the hide bitten right through, the bags of peanuts that I kept for the bird feeders ripped open, and peanuts scattered everywhere. These were mighty squirrels, and they had a tremendous appetite. It was the same with the bird feeders – the clever squirrels would bite through the rope where they were hung, high up between two trees, drop the feeders and carry them off. It was a nuisance, and was costing me a lot of money in wasted peanuts. So I took along some bags full of waste sunflower seed and maize which I get from my neighbour Jeremy. He breeds parrots, and always keeps around ten of them, so he gets through a lot of seed; and the seed that the parrots drop on the floor of their cages he sweeps up, then he bags it and gives it to me.

I spread the waste parrot seed on the ground, hoping that would give the squirrels plenty to do. It attracted pheasants, which came waddling out of the oak wood in twos and threes to peck it up. Small birds liked it too, hopping about and pecking at it, and diving down into a heap of old branches I'd left under the hide every now and again when they thought there might be a sparrowhawk watching. But it didn't really stop the squirrels attacking the hide. They preferred peanuts to parrot's maize.

I tried all sorts of solutions, but the only thing that worked was to build the squirrels their own special big box, with peanuts and maize inside and five holes for them to come and go. They spent so much time squabbling in their box that they forgot to attack the hide and the bird feeders; and they were very funny to watch, too.

Goldfinches at the hide near Twitchen

Some of the birds got used to coming to the feeders quite quickly, but others took months. It was April before the first pair of nuthatches, scarce woodland birds, came to feed on the peanuts. The woodpecker builds in a hole in a tree, and the nuthatch will do the same. But instead of simply flying in and out of the hole, once its chicks have hatched the nuthatch will adjust the size of the entrance, carefully plastering it up with mud until the hole is just big enough to feed the chicks through, but small enough to protect them from predators. Then when the chicks have grown and they're ready to fly away, the parent bird will pick away at the mud to make the hole bigger again. The nuthatch might not be as famous as

Blue tit, Bishops Nympton

the woodpecker, but it makes a better job of looking after its nest.

At home I was keeping the garden bird feeders well topped up with peanuts as well, and in early March I cleaned out the nesting boxes, so that the birds could get a fresh start. One of my commonest visitors is the blue tit. It's very pretty. When I was young I always thought the great tit was father of the blue tit, because he's so much bigger, but it's important not to confuse them – they're two separate birds, though they look nearly alike. The blue tit lays up to seven eggs in one nest.

One day in early spring I was watching two blue tits making up to each other in the garden at home, going in and out of the box where they'd nested for the past three years. As they were flying in and out, a jenny wren sneaked into the box. There was such a cheeping and chirping and distress when the tits found that the wren had got into their box, you couldn't help but smile. What the tits didn't realise was that the wren wasn't trying to take their nesting-box away from them at all – she was just going in after the insects which hide inside it.

I've never yet seen a wren nest in a box. I've seen them nest in an old kettle, or behind a tractor's seat. I've even known a wren nest in a church porch, building with moss on top of the swallow's muddy nest from the year before. Wrens like somewhere sheltered: they'll build under a fallen-down tree, at the root end, where they can be sure of shelter and cover, and can be near the ground. But the blue tits would get their box back, I was sure of that.

The winter that I built my hide at Twitchen I put up a lot of nesting boxes in the woods there. I made small boxes for tits, big ones for tawny owls, long ones with the hole near the top for woodpeckers; and I made sure that they mainly faced north or east, out of the direct sunshine. So as not to put the birds off I've always made nesting boxes out of wood from old palettes, instead of using freshly sawn wood with its strong smell. Within a fortnight of my putting them up, five of the new boxes at the hide were occupied.

Boxes will work for some birds, but others will never come near one, though they'll use other building sites. I've seen a sparrowhawk build in an old crow's nest in a thorn tree, and I've even filmed a peregrine falcon, a beautiful, wild and scarce bird, which I followed once for five years, and which built its nest on a rocky ledge in a quarry, at a secret and protected location. It's fantastic to watch the peregrine, one of our fastest birds of prey, as it kills on the wing, dive-bombing another bird in flight, so that all you see is a burst of feathers in the air as it takes its victim.

In the spring of the year on the eastern moor, the hawthorn trees come out in white or red blossom at Easter time. This is where, if you're lucky, you might see the hen harrier, a very big bird, gliding along above the moors on its wide black-tipped wings very low, three or four feet above the ground, looking for a nesting site, or

Buzzard in conifer tree

suddenly twisting in the air and diving down into the heather onto its prey. Hawks are shy and wild, and they prefer to nest high up in secret places. Once when I was a lumberjack I was felling some fir trees, and by accident I felled a buzzard's nest. Fir trees have dense branches all the way up, and it's hard to see what's in them. But I felt sorry when I looked into the nest where it lay on the ground and saw four chicks inside, all white and covered with down, looking up at me and cheeping loudly. I took three of them to Ilfracombe Zoo, and kept one myself.

I had an old ferrets' box in the garden, and that was where I put my buzzard chick. Feeding it was time-consuming: I would pull dead starlings along on a piece of string to get the buzzard to attack and eat them. Starlings were thought of as a pest in those days, because there were so many of them. It was a strange method of feeding, but it seemed to work: I reared that buzzard until it was full-grown.

When it was big I let it go so that it could get its own way of living. It flew out of its box and up to the council houses opposite our house in the village, and then sat there on the roof. And there it stayed for two or three days before flying away.

Afterwards I heard that Wally Snell, a farmer at Avercombe Farm, a quarter of a mile down the road from my house in Bishops Nympton, had suddenly started being followed by a young buzzard. It flew after him around the fields when he was out on his tractor, and when he was ploughing it used to circle round him in the sky. The buzzard chick that I reared stayed in Bishops Nympton for 16 years.

When I was a boy I used to collect birds' eggs, like a lot of other lads did. It's illegal to take eggs from nests these days, but it wasn't breaking the law back then. If you only took one egg out of the nest, the bird wouldn't notice and would carry on sitting, and rear the rest. Once I even got a swans' egg. Swans can be tricky: a swan defending its nest could break your arm. The day I took a swans' egg, I went with someone who had an Alsatian dog, to defend me from the parent birds.

Swans turning and watching their eggs

Once when I was very young my father was working in a graveyard when he called me over and told me to come out of the front gate. Then he took me up the road to the vicarage hedge.

'Look at this, boy,' he said, parting the branches in the hedge. 'I've been watching this nest for quite a long time now.' It was the nest of a hedge-sparrow, one of the smallest of our birds, and inside there was just one big chick filling the nest right up. The chick was bulging out of the nest, it was so big.

I was amazed. 'What's that?' I asked.

'That is the cuckoo. Keep quiet, we'll wait here, and in a moment we'll see the hedge-sparrow come and feed it,' said my dad. A moment later, sure enough, I saw the parent hedge-sparrow fly into the hedge with a beak full of insects. The chick was so big that the hedge-sparrow had to stand on its back to feed it. I'd never seen anything like it.

'Do you understand about the cuckoo?' said my dad.

'No,' I said, 'I don't.'

'Well,' he said, 'it lays in other birds' nests, and as it grows it gets rid of all their eggs, so the parent birds take care of the cuckoo chick instead.'

Most people know how the cuckoo uses the nests of other birds, leaving them to rear its chicks. Because it doesn't have to worry about nest-building and chick-rearing, it can afford to lay lots of eggs, up to 14 in different nests. The cuckoo chick is usually the first to hatch. It's strong and clever, and it knows how to push the other eggs out of the nest, fooling the parents into feeding it as one of their own. In the end, it's the only chick left.

Since that lesson from my father, I've always followed the cuckoo. Every year in early April I go to the moors, and the cuckoo has never failed yet. Very often in Poldhouse Combe you'll hear two or three of them, calling and answering down the valley. If you sit down and wait under a hawthorn tree, and you're lucky, you'll see the cuckoo, though it's very shy. It's hard to spot, because it's like a sparrowhawk in markings, with black and white specks, but it's quicker in flight. I've spent hours sitting under the thorn trees, waiting for a good shot of one. But so far I haven't succeeded.

In churchyards and around farm buildings in spring you'll hear the rooks noisily calling from their big rookeries as they build their nests. The early skylarks sing, and May brings the swallows, to chase the black mayfly which swarm on the moor in their thousands.

Once up on the moor I walked straight into a big flock of golden plover, two hundred of them or more. They rose up into the air when they saw me coming, turning and displaying themselves in flight. Golden plover are very, very shy, and they always come in front of the cold weather. You mostly find them on the high moor where it's damp, but it's usually a job to see them, so I was lucky. For four or five minutes I filmed these lovely birds as they swept through the air together doing their acrobatics, their feathers flashing white in the sun. It was a moment I shan't forget.

Even in the villages the nesting birds leave their mark. Once in Bishops Nympton my friends Gordon and Lorraine up the road noticed a robin starting to nest in a conifer tree outside their house.

'Johnny,' Gordon said to me one day, 'you'll never guess what's happened. That robin's forsaken its nest in the conifer, and it's gone into the garden shed to build now.'

Gordon had an open shed, where he'd piled up some old things including a cornflakes bowl and a baking tray, and a blackbird had been building there. Although the robin is three times smaller than the blackbird, it can be vicious, and will fly down at you without fear, whereas the blackbird is shy and slow. This robin had decided that the shed was a better place to build than the conifer tree, being nice and cosy and out of the weather, and it had driven the blackbird away and settled down in the cornflakes bowl.

'It's using the baking tray for a roof,' Gordon told me. 'And it's laid two eggs already.'

There had been a bit of a problem with the water pipes at Gordon's end of the village, and that same week the men from the Water Board arrived to begin digging a big trench in the road right past his house. But they hadn't reckoned with the nest in the cornflakes bowl.

'There's a robin in my shed, sitting on eggs,' Gordon explained to them. 'If you dig here now you'll disturb her and she'll forsake the nest. You've got to wait three or four weeks, and then come back when then the birds have flown away.' The men from the Water Board didn't argue.

Spring is when the weather gives up its harsh winter edge and turns soft and mild, when greenery covers the land, and the bushes everywhere begin to sprout. If I'm out stalking I can chew on very young beech leaves, or soursap leaves; or what we call bread and cheese, a tiny short plant like clover that grows in the hedgerow. This is when siskins arrive, flocks of little yellowy-green birds that many people mistake for greenfinches, though they're sleeker and smaller, with a V on their tails, and the cock has a blackish head. The siskins spend the summer in South Devon, but they always stop on Exmoor in the spring, to feed on the moor before going on further south. The reed bunting calls, the sun brings out the rabbit, and the cock pheasants protect their flocks of ten hens or more, confronting each other head-to-head to protect their territory. To them it's a serious thing.

Using a remote control to stalk and film

Foxgloves near Blackmoor Gate

Vixen with her suckling cubs, Coombe Wood near Anstey Common

Years ago when I worked as a lumberjack, bluebells and foxgloves would spring up and take hold of the wood where we cut down the trees. On Exmoor we say that the foxglove flowers when the cubs are playing around the den. The cubs grow up for weeks underground until the warm weather brings them out, and there's nothing better than watching them. A vixen will usually have three or four cubs, but it can be as many as six.

Filming the fox is difficult, and filming a vixen and her cubs is even harder, because they're so wild and wary. I need all my stalking skills to creep up on a vixen and her cubs and film them without her noticing.

There are many foxes' dens on Exmoor, though you have to know how to see them. Once I've found a den, and seen the signs that tell me there's a vixen and cubs there, I'll wait, never allowing the wind to blow from me to them. All wild animals can scent a human being, and they'll just stay underground if they think they're being watched.

You need to wait hours if you want to see the foxes play. Once I spent five and a half hours lying by a den, making sure the wind was towards me and waiting for a vixen to come back to her cubs with her kill. The cubs were out and about nearby, and I waited so long that they went to sleep twice before she returned. I watched her come back with a poult pheasant and give it to them to play with, I watched her go away again on her journey. But the moment when she came back and let them all suckle right in front of my camera made all the hours of patience worth it.

In early spring the salmon begin to run, coming in from the sea up the Exmoor rivers to spawn in the cold, shallow waters high up on the moors. The sea trout arrive next, smaller than the salmon, and different, with their distinctive square tails unlike the salmons V-shaped one; and on 1 March the fishing season begins.

My friend George is a dab hand with a worm and hook. He goes fishing on the Torridge and Lyn rivers, and he seems to have a knack of dangling the worm right down by the salmon's face, and getting him to take it. Line fishing is an expensive pastime once you've paid for the licence, but it's worth it for George. Most times he goes out, he comes back with a salmon.

For a fisherman it's good to see the high water all shiny. They know then that they're more likely to get a catch, when the sea trout are running as the evenings lengthen and it's the fishermen, out on a spring evening, who are most likely to see the otter, the shyest animal on all of Exmoor. He's so good at hiding, so secretive and so quick, that you need to stay very alert if you're to notice him at all. Many people who go fishing on the moor never see an otter in all their lives.

The otters of Exmoor like to live in the Lyn and Taw rivers, where the Tarka Trail runs. The high moorland bridges, Landacre Bridge and Head Bridge, are some of their favourite places. But they travel long distances, up to seven miles a night, and regularly change their territory, so you might see them anywhere.

WESTERN DAILY PRESS

Otters

Our two native snakes, female adder (left) and grass snake (right)

Our two native snakes, the adder and the grass snake, live on the high moor too. They like to lie coiled in the heather there, in a sheltered spot under the wind. I can't say that I like snakes. When I've filmed them, I've had such nightmares afterwards that I've woken up screaming and shouting in my sleep. They always give me the shivers; but I still try and film them. They're rare creatures, and it's something that people don't often see.

But you do have to be careful with them. Snakes go to sleep in the winter, but in the early spring, when they're coming out of hibernation, they're drowsy and confused, and will strike at anything small. Both the grass snake and the adder will bite; but the grass snake's bite is harmless. It's only the adder that will inject you with poisonous venom while it's biting.

It's easy to identify an adder. It's normally about 18 inches long, mid or dark brown in colour, with a black zigzag down its back and a V for viper on its head. A grass snake is much longer and paler, with a yellowish collar at the base of his head. He feeds mainly on frogs, while the adder eats small mammals which it stings beforehand, and then swallows whole, unlocking its jaws to slide its mouth right around its prey. Normally it keeps its fangs folded back under, but they come out when it strikes.

Once a chap told me that he had grass snakes living under the patio of his house. He lived at Whitechapel Manor, a woodland area planted with conifers. Although I don't really understand snakes at all, I know that they like somewhere to hide – a hollow in the ground, a rock – and that they like fir woods, because the spreading roots of conifer trees suit them better than the deep roots of the oak and ash.

So I took my camera and off I went, but somehow I had no luck. Although I found two dry snake skins, there was no sign of the living snakes, although the man next door told me that he often saw them leaving the house to go and eat frogs and toads at the nearby pond. Three or four times I went back, at different times of the day – but I still saw nothing.

I was puzzled until someone in the pub that night pointed out that the snakes could probably smell me. 'They smell the air with their tongues. They're very sensitive,' he said. I thought he was joking, until I realised that the wind had been in the wrong direction every day.

I hadn't honestly thought that snakes were like other wild animals in that way. But the next day I made sure I approached the place from a different direction; and I quickly saw that he'd been right. Before very long a whole snake family came came out from under the patio – two big ones, about six feet long, and several smaller ones. I shivered as I got so close so that I could see their yellow collars, and the texture of the skin on the two biggest ones, all rough and scaly, like a crocodile's.

I took two lots of film that day of 15 minutes each. When the snakes had gone, I went to a corner of the patio and lifted up a slab, and there was an adder, all curled up. I put the stone back gently. You have to be very careful with wood adders.

As the days get warmer and April turns to May, you might be lucky and spot the shy roe deer and its babies. It likes to shelter in mild nooks and crannies, in out-of-the way corners of leafy woodland valleys where it can hide, or in gorse bushes. I love the roe deer: they're so small, barely three feet high, with little black noses and needle-fine, pale brown coats. The roe deer is nothing like the red deer. It's very tiny and scarce, with tracks that are just over half the size of the red deer's. Its hoof is so miniature that you could confuse its tracks with those of a sheep quite easily, except that the sheep have blunt toes, while the roe deer's are pointy, with the slot between the hooves two finger-widths apart.

Nine times out of ten the roe doe will have twins, but they're delicate little things, and often she doesn't manage to rear both babies, and just finishes up with one. The roe fawn is a very, very small thing, and difficult to find, but you can't mistake it: it has white spots in lines down its back, and a black ring around its nose, and it's so dainty that its legs are no thicker than my finger. It'll lie very still in a tiny nest the doe digs with her feet in the leaves on the woodland floor, a little wider than a football. If you find roe fawns on their own, you should keep well away. Their mother will likely come back to them, and in any case you probably wouldn't be able to help them: a roe fawn is so delicate, it's almost impossible to rear.

To see the fawns when the mother doe cautiously brings them out into the sunshine for the first time is a very pretty thing. From my hide I've watched how they play, skipping and dancing, so small they're not much bigger than the hare. I'd love to make a film just about the roe deer.

Roe fawn near Sandy Way north of South Molton

Dormouse

Stoat

When winter ends the farmer waits for dry weather, and as soon as he can he goes out with fertiliser, manure or dung, and ploughs up the ground, works it down and tills it. During dung spreading you always get some spilt in country lanes, and spring is the time when people start complaining about their cars getting dirty.

Once years ago my sister Julie and I were walking along a lane in the spring of the year. That day the farmer had just been spreading fertiliser, and there were still lumps of dung in the road. Julie kicked one of them aside with her foot, and we were both surprised to see it break open. There inside, curled up and squeaking, was a little dormouse. One of the scarcest of our mice, it was not happy to be woken up from its long winter snooze by being kicked across the road. It scurried into the grass under the hedge and disappeared.

A lane can be a good place to find other animals too. Many people have had the experience of driving along when something's shot out in front of them on the road. Mostly they just think, 'I wonder what that was?' and carry straight on without stopping. If they did stop, they might be surprised.

Once it was a warm May day, thundery and close with the sun shining, and I was driving on my way past Sheepwash Farm up a steep hill, when all of a sudden I saw a stoat appear out of the long grass under the hedge, run straight across the road in front of me and vanish into the grass on the other side.

'Cor, flip me, I'd love to film a thing like that,' I thought. So I reversed the truck and parked at an angle across the lane, and lay in the hedge with my camera. I wouldn't advise anyone else to stop traffic to film a stoat, but that's what you have to do to get these kind of shots.

A few moments later, out came the stoat again, right beside my feet. The camera was off-balance and my hand was shaking, but I managed to keep dead still as out came another, and then another, four of them, all very young, leaping about and doing acrobatics right in front of my eyes. I'd never seen anything like it. For twenty minutes I lay there and filmed as the stoats danced, before they went away again into the grass. It was a miracle shot.

Not long afterwards I saw another group of stoats on the same part of the road. This time it was the whole family, the mother in front and the five babies running after her. They crossed the road in front of me, so close that I could see the black tip on her tail and hear her chirping to her young ones, as if to say, 'Let's go, let's go, there's danger here.' They all piled down a storm drain by the side of the road, and disappeared. The babies must have been born down there, because they knew exactly where to go. Their pale winter coats were spotted with the darker brown that they would wear during the long summer months ahead.

SUMMER

Summer is the time when all of life is on the go, from the biggest animals to the smallest; and it's the best time to visit the woodlands of Exmoor. You hear the birdsong more clearly then, the call of the wood warbler, or the chiffchaff's high sharp note. The young buzzard calls from its nest, and far away there's the sound of the woodpecker, chipping and drilling at the trees; and where the rivers flow beneath the valleys, you'll see the dragonflies hovering above the water. If you go to the woods on a still evening, walking very quietly with the wind in the right direction, you might hear the snorting and squeaking of badger cubs playing among the trees.

It's mostly oaks that grow in the valleys, with ash and some beech. Five Cross Way, just off Anstey Common, is famous for its avenues of tall beeches. On the scrubland, further up the moor, there's hawthorn, and willow-withy, as we call it –

STEVE GUSCOTT

Heather on Molland Moor in the peak of summertime

and the high beech hedges that you don't see anywhere else but Exmoor; and by the hot days of July the heather's in bloom, and the high moor is all in purple.

Summer brings good pickings in the fields and woods. I've often found field mushrooms in the summer, pale, flat and white, and taken them home to fry in a pan. The best are the button mushrooms, small and young, and usually maggot-free, though as with all wild food, it's best to check. In the hedgerows there are small, sweet wild strawberries; then later, blackberries and hazelnuts.

Every summer in Bishops Nympton we have a revels week, a seven-day stretch when there's always something doing.

One of the week's biggest attractions is the old custom of beating the bounds, when the whole village walks and marks the boundary of the parish. Our parish is a big one, and the boundary's too far to walk in one go; so every year we walk a different section, carrying a pot of white paint to mark the bounds, or following the marks of the year before; and we always finish at a pub, with a pint, or a cup of tea and biscuits. It's a good night out which the whole village enjoys. Lots of people turn out for the walk, 70 or 80 of us, adults and children, and dogs on leads, though it's not an easy course, following rivers and fences, going through fields and under trees. Michael Warren leads the way, and my job is to control the children. It was difficult to start with: I had to explain about shutting gates when we walked across farmers' land, and thanking the farmer. But the children are good when you get to know them, and over the years I've grown to like them all.

The month of June is very important for the red deer, because the first and second weeks are the main time for calving. It's not easy to find a newborn deer calf; you have to get out very early in the morning, find a good spot, and carefully watch the hinds' movements. A hind will choose a special place to hide to have her calf, and it will probably be very well-hidden. The calf gets on its legs as soon as it's born, and the mother will lick it off straight away, and then feed it. That first bit of milk with its calcium is very important for her baby, and it will suckle and then lie down quietly. After that the mother hind will wander away, so as not to draw attention to her calf's hiding place; and she won't come back to it until the following evening. She'll

Frog sitting on my arm, beating the bounds, Bishops Nympton

Four stags in velvet near Ringcombe

Newborn deer calf, not far from Bishops Nympton

Newborn deer calf near Molland village

keep doing this for more than a week, until the baby is fit to follow her.

Many deer calves are born in the fields, in the long grass that's mown for hay in the month of June. Nowadays the mowing machines are so big that they can easily destroy a little thing like a newborn deer calf that's been carefully hidden by its mother in the middle of the field. Often the farmer will come across the calf, but there are times when he can't stop the machine before it's too late.

Luckily many calves are also born in the woods. One year I decided to film one, though it took me nearly a week of hard stalking and careful watching to find it. Although the calf couldn't see me, because I was well camouflaged, even at two days old its sensitive nose moved as it tried to scent me. But it was too young to be afraid. To take pictures naturally like this, with the calf not knowing you're there – that's what wildlife filming is all about, for me.

It's very important not to separate a deer calf from its mother. At calving time you find many abandoned on the moors, where the hind has been disturbed, and has run away and left her calf behind.

Once some years ago near the village of Molland, a well-known farmer, Brian Buckingham, was checking his stock when he found a tiny fawn caught in a wire

My granddaughter Roxy feeding Bambi

Bambi, two weeks old, before she had her leg taken off.

fence, hanging upside down by one leg. Knowing I take care of the wildlife, he rang me up early in the morning of 7 June in 1996, my wife Julie's birthday.

'I haven't got the nerve to destroy it, Johnny, and I don't know what to do,' he said. 'It's tried to follow its mum over a hedge, and it's got its leg caught in the wire. It's no more than three days old, I reckon.'

I came round straight away. The calf was very, very tiny and dainty, with little white spots on her back, and so weak and small that she could barely stand up. I picked her up and brought her home, and we called her Bambi. The wound on her leg didn't look too good, so I called Martin Prior, a very good local vet, to check her over. He gave her a 50-50 chance of survival because she was so small.

If I wanted Bambi to survive, the first thing I had to do was find a way of feeding her. The milk for a baby deer calf is a very, very important thing. If you feed them cows' milk they only have a rare chance of living, because it's too rich for them. What they need is goat's milk. Luckily my friend Jill Wollacott came to the rescue. She rears goats, and I was able to feed Bambi every three hours round the clock with fresh milk from one of her animals.

Two weeks later Bambi's leg had turned very nasty, so Martin the vet came again. 'I'm sorry, Johnny, but the foot's dead. I'm going to have to take her leg completely off,' he said.

Soon after the operation the phone rang, with good news – Bambi had survived the operation, and was wide awake. 'But you'd better come in, Johnny,' Martin said. 'She's hollering for her mother, and I think that means you.' I went to the surgery straight away. As I got out of the truck I could hear her loud distress cries, and there she was, lying in a little pen, wrapped in bandages with one of her back legs missing. I lay down next to her in the straw, and she pushed her head against me and gradually stopped crying. We rested a while together like that, and then I brought her home.

Julie was very upset to see Bambi without her leg, and it was a big nursing job for both of us to take care of her until she grew stronger. I still had to feed her with the goat's milk every three hours, day and night, until after a week or two she perked up and started hobbling about on her three legs, and the whole family could join in with feeding her.

A tame three-legged hind wouldn't survive long in the wild; so we decided to keep Bambi permanently. Bringing her up was hard, though. It took some sacrifices: my wife had to give up her lawn, and now the back garden is one big mud wallow. You can't blame Bambi – it's natural deer behaviour to roll in mud, and it does her good. She rubs her head against our conifer trees, and that's normal too. At one side I've built her a shelter which is always clean and dry; and to keep her free of ticks I go round the sawmills and collect sawdust for her bed, rather than giving her hay or straw.

Bambi eats two bags of good-quality coarse calf feed every three weeks. I cut her toenails regularly, and in the spring I always give her shaggy winter coat a thorough combing, to help bring out the shiny coat of summer.

WESTERN DAILY PRESS

Bambi full-grown

My granddaughters Roxy and Louise still help us look after Bambi, and I've made a film about her too. Many people know about her, and a lot of my neighbours help take care of her. Every single day Joe Drewer, who lives at the top of my road, puts a bag of tatty peelings – potato peelings – inside my gate for her, and he looks after her when we're on holiday. Sometimes a kind neighbour will leave other peelings too: apple, maybe, or carrot. Ron Atkins always brings her bags of windfall apples in the summertime, and Cath and Richard down at the grocer's shop save waste bread for her. Bambi always loves seeing visitors, and she eats all the food they bring. Custard cream biscuits are her favourite, though she doesn't get them very often. Wherever I go, people always ask how Bambi is. She means a lot to us: she's a symbol of the wild, and she's one of the family as well.

Beautiful stags in velvet

Deer calves grow quickly. After a few weeks they're already out with their mothers in the herd, hinds and calves together with a few stags as well, feeding in the woods, moors and fields in the warmth of the summer sun. The hinds are very proud of their babies, and very alert, and even at a very young age the calves' ears are pricked for the slightest danger. Although you could easily mistake them for deer in a park, they're wild creatures, and they'll run away quickly if they feel threatened.

By midsummer, when the oats and barley are standing high in the fields, the stags have half-grown their new antlers. They're

Hinds and calves at the bottom of Anstey valley

still rubbery and soft, covered in a fuzzy soft dark coat called velvet, and they bleed easily if they're knocked. When the ferns start to grow on the moor, so do the antlers; and we always say that when the ferns are fully grown, the antlers will be too. It takes three months to grow a full new set of antlers. While it's happening the deer spend a lot of time lying in the fields in the sun, just quietly chewing their cuds, all together, shaking their antlers against the hundreds of flies which always seem to gather round their heads.

They don't just help themselves to the farmer's crops all the time, as some people think. Once I lay in a field at Ringcombe near Anstey from 2 o'clock in the afternoon until 7.15 in the evening, filming a group of stags in velvet as they fed from the young leaves of trees in a hedgerow. They were huge, proud animals, with a full head of velvet, and although they were wild, when they all lined up to nibble the tasty leaves they looked just like a row of cows feeding from a rack in a cowshed. It was lovely to see them stretch their whole seven or eight-foot lengths up into the hedge to reach the smallest, tenderest leaves.

Poldhouse Combe is one of my favourite places for stalking deer. I'm almost guaranteed to see them there, especially in the summer months. It was on Poldhouse Combe, one very warm evening right in the peak of the summer months, that I was lucky enough to film one of the best stags on Exmoor, with all his rights and six on one side, and brow, bay, trey, and four on the other. As I drew very close with my camera the stag lifted his head and proudly looked me right in the eye. By the time I had finished filming him seven or eight Land Rovers had drawn up on the moor above to watch us. Everyone likes to see a fine stag on the moor.

With their antlers in velvet the stags look at their best, in July and August before the circulation of blood to the antler slows down and it begins to dry up. Often towards the end of the summer months you'll see a magpie pitch down on the back of a deer, to pick off the insects and ticks from the back of its body.

Stags reaching for, and eating, hazel leaves in the summertime at Ringcombe

Stags in velvet with a magpie

Ticks cause Lyme disease, which is dangerous to stalkers and walkers as well as tormenting the deer; so the magpie's doing a useful job by eating them.

As the summer ripens the stags seek out the high moorland, where the Exmoor ponies graze and the heather and gorse grow, so that they can start ripping all their velvet off on the stiff, spiky gorse bushes, and sharpening their antlers ready to defend themselves during the autumn rutting season.

One late summer's day in 2001, when foot and mouth disease closed so much of the moorland, I spent a whole afternoon crawling on my stomach with the wind towards me, up towards the main road on Soakey Moor, not far from Anstey Common. From a distance I'd seen 14 or 15 stags in velvet.

The ground was very wet, and it didn't take long before I was soaked. The stags were sitting down, russet brown in the purple heather, chewing the cud and flicking their heads against the flies. I crawled out to get as close as I could, and when I was within 50 yards I stopped and set up the camera so that I could film myself going closer. Then I crawled on, and when I got to within 20 yards I very slowly stood up. 'Hello, what are you doing up there?' I said quietly to the deer. I often talk gently to the animals just at the moment when I begin to film them. It gives me a few extra seconds when they're interested and puzzled, before they decide to head off and run away. As the stags were getting up I got my shot — a pair of stags with their antlers together like a tripod. What do you want prettier than that, I thought.

While the deer are on the moor rubbing at their antlers, the badgers are busy in the valleys, getting as much food as they can before the coming winter. I appreciate the badgers, but they don't have a good reputation with everyone. Even though many farmers like them, I know that they can become a menace. When they get into a cornfield in the early summer, and play together, they'll ruin a wide area of corn by rolling it completely flat. Or they'll dig their sett under a field, making big hollows, which is lethal for a tractor if the ground's soft. The law to make these animals a protected species was brought in years ago, and their numbers may have got out of hand by now.

But the badger can be useful too; and as long as he's living in rough ground where nobody has to drive a vehicle, he causes no real harm. Unlike the fox, he doesn't take lambs, living mainly on slugs and worms.

Some years ago it was thought that badgers with TB passed the disease on to cattle. But although thousands of badgers have been destroyed, no connection has ever been established between bovine and badger TB. I've always found the badger to be harmless in himself. To see him standing on his hind legs, with his paws in a honey pot, even licking his nails afterwards, how could anybody believe that he's a bad animal?

He's strong in his own way, and he can be very fierce. One sunny

A very rare shot of two stags forming a tripod

Stalking stags in velvet on Soakey Moor near Molland Moor

Stag losing velvet on Molland Moor

Badger feeding on peanuts and honey

summer evening I was driving down from the moor into the Barle Valley when I heard a tremendous screeching noise, and stopped the car to see two boar badgers fighting. They must have been arguing over territory, an important thing for any animal.

In some ways the badger can be very predictable. He needs to drink, and he'll walk a long way to a river or stream, always taking the same route. It's the same with his foraging habits, when he goes out looking for slugs and insects, and digging into the earth with his nose for worms and beetles – he'll always follow the same track. He's often bound to cross a road on his travels, and the last thing on his mind is traffic. Many badgers are killed on the Exmoor roads.

The summer months are when the birds rear their half-grown chicks, and finding the food to do it keeps them busy all day long. The chaffinch, one of our more common birds, builds a neat cup-shaped nest lined with horsehair and fine mossy lichen. One year I went to my friends Sid and Mary Payne's farm near Roach Hill, where I could get very, very close to the nest of a chaffinch set in an ivy-covered wall.

It's tricky filming young birds. Like all wild creatures, chaffinches are shy and easily disturbed. The last thing you want is for them to get frightened and forsake the nest, because then all the chicks die. So I had to be careful. I buried my camera in a camouflage net and stayed very still and peaceful, dressed in camouflage gear myself and with a camouflage net over my head. It took many days, but I got my shot in the end.

It was a similar problem when a spotted flycatcher built under a ledge in a wall in the village. It was mid-July by now, and the weather was warm and sunny. The spotted flycatcher with its sharp cry and quick flight is the last bird in the year to build, making a small, cup-like nest in a wall, a shed or a garden, but always on a ledge under cover. It feeds its chicks only on insects, and because it nests too late for the mayfly you'll often see it flying in to pitch down on the nest with a butterfly in its beak, like a moving flower. It took many days' watching before I got my shot.

Years ago gypsies were an everyday sight on Exmoor. They walked along the side of the road with their horses pulling fancy caravans, or you'd see them pulled over, camped by the road with their horses. They lived all the way round the villages, in the lanes and laybys, in strong, loyal families. The men dealt in scrap iron, and the women told fortunes and made things to sell. They were always dressed smartly – if you saw a gipsy in a pub he'd be wearing a trilby hat and a waistcoat, with a gold watch chain dangling from his pocket watch. He was the type of person who would always buy you a drink.

In my schooldays, when I used to collect birds' eggs, I was friends with a boy from a gipsy family. His name was Raymond, and he used to live in an old-fashioned caravan with an oval-shaped roof in Gipsy Lane at Aller Cross, smartly painted in bright red and green, with red wheels. You went up some steps to go inside, where behind the living quarters there were bunk beds at the back, and outside some horses would always be tied up nearby, cropping the grass.

In those days there were many curlews on Exmoor, though they've become scarce since the farmers started using pesticide sprays. Raymond always knew where the curlews laid, out on the rough land in clumps of rushes. The eggs looked something like a seagull's in colour, the same buff

Chaffinch's nest at Sid and Mary Payne's farm

Spotted flycatcher at its nest, the vicarage, Bishops Nympton

colour with dark spots, but pointier than the seagull's. It was always hard to find the nests, because the bird would circle in the air and never approach its eggs if we were there; and we knew that if there were babies, the parent bird might attack us with its long, curved, sharp beak. But the high, haunting note of the curlew's call across the open moor was one of the most beautiful sounds of my boyhood.

There used to be many herons on Exmoor too, but they've become more scarce now that so many wetlands have been drained and there are fewer fish. Some of the old heronries are still there, though, colonies in tall trees where the birds lay their eggs on flat platforms of sticks so thin that in some places you can see right through them if you look up. Herons lay sky-blue eggs the size of a chicken's. They make a lovely chuckling sound when they come in to land on their nest, and to see them feeding their young is fantastic – they fill the pouch under their beak with fish, pitch down on the nest and then regurgitate the fish straight into their babies' open beaks.

Heron in spring

Fish are eaten by some of Exmoor's prettiest birds. If you're walking in the summer by the upper reaches of the Barle you might catch sight of the kingfisher, a blue flash like lighting on the river. I've seen him strike in the water, come up a moment later with a minnow, and swallow it whole, head first; but it's a moment I've never managed to film, it happens so fast.

The Barle rises at Pinkery Pond, high up on the moors near Simonsbath, and it runs right over Exmoor, falling into the Exe below Dulverton. On a fine day on the river you'll likely see the dipper bird as he dips and dips, then dives right underneath the water, coming up with a minnow in his beak. He's a shy bird, not widely known; but he's been living on the Barle as long as I remember.

This is where the kingfishers nest, drilling holes with their beaks 14 inches deep in the clay banks of the upper reaches of the river, half a mile up from Landacre Bridge towards Challacombe. You can tell a kingfisher's hole by the little heaps of fishbones outside, and the bank below the hole whitewashed with droppings. But the kingfisher is a protected bird, and you mustn't go near the nest.

At Marsh Bridge on the Barle I've filmed dippers quite a few times. The water up here on the high moors is as clear as gin, not mucky like the river water of the valley below. It's rich in fish, and you can guarantee a few trout most of the time. One sunny day when our children were small we came for a picnic here, and brought along five other boys from the village for a day out. We had nothing with us to eat except bread and butter, a calor gas stove and a frying pan. That day I got in the river and tickled enough trout to give everybody one each for dinner. We cleaned them in the river and cooked them in batter, flour and water, there on the river bank. That day we ate the freshest food there is.

Kingfisher and sand martins' nesting site, Barle River

WESTERN DAILY PRESS

Landacre Bridge

Tickling trout can get you into trouble. One hot summer day when I was a boy, a gang of us went down to the river across a field from where Uncle Harry Moule lived. Knowing me, I was soon up to my belly in a corner of the water, hoping to tickle a trout. I got on my knees, put my hand in the water and straight away I could feel a fish – but I was puzzled by the strange hole that I kept touching in the side of his belly. I kept putting my finger in the hole and feeling how soft it was, when all of a sudden my finger disappeared right into it, and I realised that what I was touching was the mouth of an eel. I quickly pulled back, but the eel's teeth, which always look backwards, had already hooked into me. The next thing I knew, I was out on the bank with a three-foot eel hanging off my finger and threshing around, and the others were trying to kill it with their bows and arrows. Mr Clark gave me two shillings for that eel.

Always you'll see swallows flying over the moor in midsummer, dipping and soaring as they chase insects through the air. House martins are smaller than swallows, although they're similar to look at. They're very clever, flying all the way from Africa to the same place every year to raise their families. A pair arrives every year at our house, to nest under the guttering of the roof. They leave an almighty mess on the ground under the nest, but we don't mind; it's good to see them here, swooping swiftly through the air in the evenings as they catch insects and flies, or screeching madly as they fly in wide circles round the house. When the house martins leave for Africa again, we know that summer's nearly over.

Sand martins build in the Barle riverbanks alongside the kingfishers. Like the

House martins nesting at my home in Bishops Nympton

Young buzzard in its nest, near the Black Cock Hotel

house martin, but brown in colour, they dig shallower holes than the kingfisher, only 8 inches deep, and live in big colonies along the clay banks. It's lovely to watch whole flocks of them skimming the water on a summer's day, flying in and out of their holes. To film them you have to be very quiet, wait peacefully, and hope to get good results.

High over the moors on a summer's day you'll see the hawks gliding, sailing silently in the air as they watch for prey: the kestrel, hen harrier, peregrine falcon and buzzard. Not far from the Black Cock Hotel on the road to Molland there's a tall beech tree 30 feet high, which I once climbed regularly for four weeks to film a buzzard's nest.

There were two eggs in the nest, one of which was addled and didn't hatch. But I followed the other chick from when it was a little baby. The buzzard hawk builds a rough, untidy nest, and will come back year after year to the same spot. Most times it lays three eggs, and usually rears three chicks. It feeds them on carrion – dead meat, often road kill – small mammals, even rabbits; and birds, including the magpie. We should take care of the buzzard, a natural predator of the magpie which attacks the farmer's lambs.

Every time I wanted to film this buzzard chick I had to climb up into the tree, often in a high wind. I had a job not to disturb it or frighten the parent birds; but it was interesting seeing the nest at close hand. It contained a jumble of things – blue string, bits of dead magpie, a lamb's tail. I followed the chick until it grew up, and it was wonderful to watch the day it took off and flew away.

Another of our native birds of prey is the barn owl. He's an attractive bird, but very, very shy, and so rare now that he's protected and you need a special licence to go and film him. They're not birds that breed very easily: often they only have one chick, but even if they have more, they rarely rear all their family. Owls fly in June, in haymaking time; but because of modern farming methods, which use sprays that kill small animals and remove their ground cover, these days it's often hard for them to find enough to eat.

Some people try and help. In the village of George Nympton there's a farmer I know who has barn owls at his place, recently set aside a two-acre strip of grass when he was cutting hay, and left it long especially so that the owls could feed on the voles. He wasn't paid anything to do it – he was just looking after the wildlife.

Swans with their cygnets in the evening

One summer evening I visited a nature reserve owned by the Barn Owl Trust to film the owls there. I was hoping we'd be lucky; and sure enough, very soon we saw one owl sitting in a tree. Just as I got the camera ready he took off from his branch and glided across the water, very still and quiet. I had no tripod, and I was just turning completely around to follow him with the camera, when suddenly he dived into the reed bed; and a moment later there he was, flying up again in the twilight, carrying a water vole in one claw. I got a clear, lovely shot of something very rarely seen. It was a beautiful moment.

The tawny owl is less well-known than the barn owl. He's a woodland bird, and likes best of all to nest in an old tree-trunk.

I built my second badger hide with nesting boxes around it, and where the boxes joined the hide I put in Perspex windows so that I could look right into the boxes and film the chicks without disturbing them. One year I was thrilled to find that some tawny owls were using one of my boxes. They laid only two eggs, of which they reared one baby. The chick seemed nice and cosy in the box, a ball of fluff sitting in the corner and eating the food – mice, voles, even squirrels – which the parents brought.

Barn owl diving onto prey in a water meadow, and with its kill, a water vole, dangling from one talon

Tawny owl chick at my hide

Female kestrel at her nest

Red-legged partridge in beech hedge

Kestrels like to build on ledges in inaccessible places. Week Farm near the village of Kings Nympton once had some kestrels build in a small quarry there, which I thought I'd try and film.

Kestrels are very watchful, and mostly you'll never get near them. I had to be very gentle and careful. I dressed up in camouflage gear, with a full camouflage mask, and gloves. I buried the camera and my whole body in netting, and lay very still to film. Over the weeks I followed the birds as they finished their nest and laid their eggs, and I watched them bring young mice and voles to the growing chicks. All went well until the chicks were half-grown, and then one day I went there to find that all the chicks had been taken. I was told that someone had stolen them. I couldn't understand why anyone would do something like that. If they'd seen how the parent birds took care of their chicks, if they'd watched them flying in and out all the time rearing them, surely they would never have destroyed them.

All over Exmoor game birds are reared throughout the year, ready for the autumn shooting season. There's big money in it, and they're an important part of Exmoor life.

By the time summer comes, the new pheasant poults are ready to leave their rearing sheds and go out into pens in the woods, to learn to live outdoors and scratch food for themselves. This is also the time when the vixens on the moor are working hard on finding food for their growing cubs, and a pen full of young

Vixen bringing back part of a pheasant for her cubs

pheasants is exactly what they're looking for. A fox in a pen of pheasants will go on a killing spree, biting the head off each one instead of taking just one to eat. A vixen will train her cubs to eat pheasants; for her it's excellent food, and foxes will take hundreds of them over one season. The fox is a menace to the game-bird keepers, and their numbers do have to be kept down.

But it would be a pity to wipe them out completely. Like all the wild animals, when you watch the fox in his natural way of living you see what a beautiful creature he is. He isn't always the loner that people imagine. I've seen a den with one litter of small cubs at one end, and a big litter at the other end, all playing together, a total of 11 cubs in one den, in two large litters. Sometimes you'll see a fox family occupying spare space at the end of a badger sett, too, and living peacefully alongside the badgers and their cubs.

June is the prettiest time. That's when you might see a young fox cub lying fast asleep in the middle of the field, or digging a bit of earth, playing, looking for something to chase: spiders, beetles, as long as it moves he doesn't mind. That's how the fox is.

By the middle of summer, when the cubs are nearly half grown, they've become very, very shy; but still, when they see my camera, they're curious and wonder what's going on. I get very close, no more than four yards away. The cub gets up and has a good stretch, then looks straight at me, and I talk to him.

Young fox cub at Ash Mill

'Hello, you pretty little thing,' I say. He doesn't run away. The thing is, he hasn't been on the earth very long. It's sad that if he's near a pheasant pen, most likely he won't stay on the earth too long either.

Summer is the time for outings to the rocky Exmoor coast. As a boy we'd go on Sunday school trips once a year to Minehead or Ilfracombe, or Bude. We were always very excited about going so far away, although my excitement wore off once when we went to Bude and found hundreds of jellyfish covering the beach, like small saucers, and I got badly stung.

But I have always liked sea fishing: my sons Stuart and Craig are rod and line boys to this day. Once I took the family out to Crow Point to fish from the rocks, in a Consul car which I'd just had resprayed. We parked on the beach and had a good time fishing, until – too late – we noticed that the tide had come in. We had no choice but to sit on the roof of the car and wait it out. It was a shame about the car, though – it was never the same again after that.

We used to enjoy sea fishing from a boat, too, once we'd got our sea legs. You can catch conger eels all round the Devon coast, black fish up to five feet long or more, with bluey-grey, big eyes, and flesh that's sweet when it's cut into steaks and fried in flour and water, though it's full of bones, not like the salmon. The conger is a strong animal, and you have to hit it hard on the tail to kill it before putting it in a big bin on the deck. Even then it'll sometimes climb out again, sneak up behind you and try to bite you with its sharp teeth.

A clear day, the kind when you can see right across the sea to Wales, is the best for fishing. You catch mackerel to start with, and then use that to catch dogfish, skate and young shark. One man in the village, Ray Setherton, always used to take my fish, especially the conger. He'd been badly wounded in the war, had lost an eye and had had dozens of operations on his face. Ray used to wear a glass eye, and because it was always dropping out and smashing, or getting damaged, he'd always order a couple of dozen glass eyes at a time. In the pub he'd make us all laugh by saying to me, 'Keep an eye on my beer, Johnny,' and then getting up from the table and dropping one of his eyes into the beer. Ray was a lovely man.

The north coast is very pretty in the summertime. This is where the razorbills nest, at Ringer's Peak looking towards Woody Bay; and the fulmer builds here, different from a seagull because it keeps its wings straight as it flies. It's very high and dangerous here: the cliffs are undermined, and you can step out near the edge thinking that you'll put your foot onto firm ground, only to find yourself falling into the sea. People have died here by taking a step too far.

One summer I'd heard that the adders had come out very early near Parracombe, not far from Countisbury Hill, in the Valley of Rocks. The valley's a dangerous spot, with cliffs 300 feet high, and it's known for ghosts and snakes. We've always been told that if you're out there alone late at night the Devil will catch you, or you might hear the hoofbeats of a swift horse carrying a White Lady coming after you.

The White Lady is just a story, but the snakes are real. I took a mate with me the day I went to film them, knowing that if I got stung he could raise the alarm. It was a very hot, still day, just the kind of weather when you're likely to see adders. The viper has a V on his head, and there's no mistake about the male – he's black and white. The female has a V on her head too, and she's marked exactly the same as the male but she's brown in colour. They can grow up to two feet in length.

We'd timed it well, and it wasn't long before I saw a snake all coiled up, in a bundle, in the leaves, sleepy from its long winter hibernation. I told my mate to stay back, and felt the shivers myself as I got within four yards of it.

As I drew closer I saw that there were three, a brown female and two black males, and I could see that they were active, and getting ready to mate. As I watched, the two males rose up and challenged each other. They were swaying and moving together as though they were hypnotised by each other, and for the first time I understood what's meant by the saying 'dancing snakes'. A strange feeling went through my whole body as I watched them. I knew I was seeing something rare and special, but I didn't know where to put myself, I was so frightened. It's easy to forget that although wildlife is nice to see, sometimes it can be dangerous.

They were big adders, around two feet long, and they moved so fast it was hard to follow them as they coiled and wriggled. Then a fourth

Male and female adders mating on Countisbury Hill

The Valley of Rocks near Lynton and Lynmouth

Mountain goat at the Valley of Rocks

adder joined them. By now one of them was actually mating with the female, joined together at the tail in the hot clifftop sunshine there on the rocks, while the others coiled around them. It was a fantastic moment to film.

For the next three and a half days I went back to film the adders, though my mate refused to return to the place after the first day. I found a rare black adder too, 300 yards away, on its own. Though by the end of it I had had my fill of snakes, I'd got some wonderful footage.

At the top of the Valley of Rocks, looking back towards Woody Bay, above Lynton and Lynmouth, there are lots of little paths. It's a lovely place to walk, and it's the home of what we call the billygoats, Exmoor's wild mountain goats.

Two hundred feet above the sea, these large animals spend their lives grazing on the sides of the cliffs. It's amazing that they don't fall. The old goats have big horns, and to see two of them fighting, crashing their horns together with a great noise, is very impressive – and it can be dangerous. Mostly the goats are very shy, hiding away on inaccessible crevices in the cliffs, happily grazing where no-one can climb up to them.

The summer warmth and good feeling brings out the roe deer, too, though they're hard to see in summer when the woods are leafy. July is the roe deer's rutting season. Unlike the red deer, it will never roar; instead, if you're lucky, you might hear its funny bark. Its antlers are much smaller – over ten inches of antler means a big buck if it's a roe deer – and it's much rarer than the red deer.

Towards Taunton, on the lower ground, you do find fallow deer as well, light in colour and scattered with white spots, with antlers flat in shape, like the palm of your hand with little sharp points. But I haven't ever heard of fallow deer up on the moor.

A young leveret having a clean-up

Years ago when I was a young boy working on Mr Tucker's farm, one of my jobs was to catch the moles which spoilt the farmer's fields with their digging. I had dozens of mole traps, which I used to set round all the farms in the area. As well as my own moles I'd take rabbits, stoats, even foxes from the trappers, skin them all out and send the skins to Horace Friend, the dealer. For a stoat you got 2s. 6d., and you could sell a fox skin for 5s. Mole skins went from a penny to a shilling each, depending what condition they were in.

In those days late summer meant harvest time, hot days when gangs of us would follow the binder, carrying sticks with clumps on the end. As the area of standing corn grew smaller and smaller you'd see the corn moving where the rabbits were hiding, and we'd catch them as they tried to escape. Once we were on Mr Tucker's farm and there was just a little strip of corn left, four feet wide, when we saw the corn move and suddenly a big rat came running out. As we went to get it with the sticks it suddenly jumped four feet in the air, grabbed my sister Julie's hand with its teeth and hung on. She was very ill after that, and had to be rushed to hospital.

As well as rabbits, hares also live in the hayfields, though they're less plentiful than they once were, now that hay meadows are managed more efficiently and cut more quickly. They're pretty to see, running wild on open ground, making a nest on the bracken or on a tuft of grass instead of going to earth as a rabbit does; and they're bigger than the rabbit, with powerful hind legs and short forepaws.

I was thrilled when I once got up to within a few yards of a young hare peacefully grooming itself, so close that I could clearly make out the black tips of its long ears. I was very, very lucky to get so close. I only managed it because the leveret was young, and didn't know much about the world.

But it would soon learn. As the high golden days of June and July turn to the ripeness of August, the animals grow fast. They know they don't have much time. In the mornings of late August, the dews are heavier and the air is colder. Though the days are still warm, Autumn is on the way.

AUTUMN

Autumn comes slowly on Exmoor, with golden days and chilly nights, and insects buzzing in the heather as they collect the last nectar of summer. This is the time of the harvest, when still today around Bishops Nympton the corn is cut with an old-fashioned binder, tying it into sheaves for stacking and drying in the fields in the warm sunshine of early September. The corn is threshed and the stem set aside, to be dried and used for house thatching, and then it's party time for the boys who worked on the harvest. As they have a big dinner together, and the fruits of the year are brought to the church for harvest festival, the autumn begins to creep in over the moors.

By mid-September the ferns are changing colour, and the heather turns brown as its small purple flowers begin to die off. About three weeks later – sooner, maybe, if there's a frost – the purple of the moors will be gone, with rusty colours on the grass and ferns of the rough open country, and quiet in the air.

As the summer ends the adult cuckoos are one of the first birds to leave for warmer places. True to form, they leave their babies behind to follow as they can. And then the martins, swallows, swifts and all the migrating birds begin to fly away from Exmoor in the changing light and early chill of autumn. This is the season when the goldfinches gather in flocks, maybe 50 at a time, to feed on the seeds of the thistle heads – dashel heads, we call them – which grow everywhere on the high ground; and the spiders spread their webs across the prickles of the gorse bushes in white nets, while down below, in the lanes and woods, all the leaves are rich in colour.

One of the most popular places with visitors is the Barle Valley underneath Hawkridge, where the loveliest season is autumn, before the winter cold sets in. Tarr Steps, an old stone packhorse bridge and ford a mile up the river, is well-loved for picnics and cream teas in the cafe, and there are miles and miles of signposted walks. This is where the foxes live, and the red deer, though at this time of year they might not always be where you expect to find them. The chill in the air at the end of summer means that the mating season, the rut, has nearly arrived; and the deer are on the move.

Tarr Steps

At the beginning of September the stags on the moor are still all living together in groups. They're beginning to think about rutting, and you'll see them working hard at rubbing their antlers on the trees to scrape away the last of the velvet, sharpening them up and getting them hard and dry. In these last days of September, their antlers are a light chocolate colour like the autumn leaves.

One of my favourite places for watching deer is Molland Moor, though you'll also find them at Anstey Common and Dunkery Beacon. On any day in early September, if I'm lucky, I might count more than 50 hinds there, some with young calves, only about a month old and still with their spots. The hinds look proud, beautifully camouflaged against the purple and grey of the heather and grass; but I'm always sorry to see the youngsters. When a calf is born so late in the year, it never survives the winter.

Stalking the stags in September, I know that they'll soon split up to claim their herds of hinds. As October approaches they begin to leave and go off on their own to find their own territories, because the last week of September running on into October is the rutting season. In the weeks leading up to the rut they go out and search for better food, too, so that they can build themselves up. By the time the rut's over, six weeks later, a stag is likely to be nothing but a bag of bones. With the urge to mate constantly on him, the need to defend his territory and the challenges from other stags day and night, he hardly has time to eat at all.

Hind near Willingford Bridge

Stag and hinds in Cloggs Valley

Stag with hinds and yearlings, Ley Hill, near Porlock

Young pricket in velvet

A stag can lose more than half his body weight during the rutting season.

October is the month when it all happens. All the stags are alert for the challenges and fights, and people gather from miles around to watch. You might get one big stag defending a herd of, say, 30 hinds, and he'll be challenged by another big stag. As they fight, you'll sometimes see all the young ones, the prickets, hanging round on the outside, watching. While the two older ones are battling it out with their sharp antlers, a young stag will often sneak in quickly and serve the hinds behind their backs. It makes me laugh, the cheek of them.

The mating instinct overtakes every other thought, and even the very young stags don't think about the danger they're in from these heavy, muscular and angry animals with a full head of horns sharpened to points as deadly as knives.

It's awesome to watch two big stags as they roar out their challenge and clash their antlers together. Even though they're so dangerous, their beauty and strength can take your breath away.

When the rutting season starts on Exmoor, the most important part of my year begins. Between the middle of September and the end of October I try not to miss a single day's filming. I'm looking for the obvious shots – the stags fighting and roaring out their challenge down the valley – but I'm always on the look-out for something unexpected too. Sometimes it isn't even deer. Once I filmed two bulls fighting – a black Angus and a Devon bull – in a field of long-coated Highland cattle for nearly twenty minutes. They were going hard at it; and what tickled me most was that at the beginning there were only about ten cows watching, but by the end there were more than a hundred. All the cows in the area had gathered to have a good look. Two chaps came along on quad bikes, and when I pointed out the bulls they laughed. 'Those are our cows,' they told me. 'They love to see a good fight. And our Angus isn't afraid of that Devon bull.'

No-one would ever go into a field where bulls are fighting; but often people don't realise that rutting stags can be just as dangerous. Between October and November the stags are worst enemies, and if you get in their way when they're fighting for territory, they'll come right at you – and a big stag can kill a man. Many's the time I've spent hours up in a tree with an angry stag below.

An angry stag will go for anything, a dog out on a walk, even a sheep. Once I was out with young John Bere and his fiancée Helen, when we started watching two stags with three or four hinds in a group. As we watched, a sheep approached, quietly nibbling the grass. 'I'm sure that stag's going to attack that sheep,' said John, amazed.

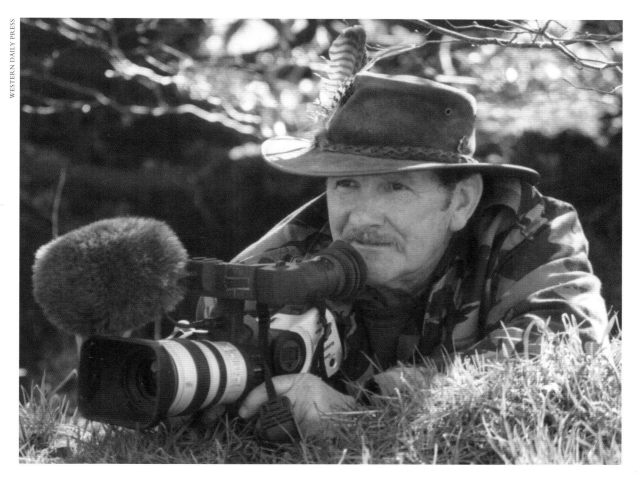

'Better get your camera out.' As we watched we saw the stag put its horns down, push them into the sheep and bowl it over twice. The poor sheep pitched down onto his feet and ran away like a rocket to the other end of the field.

But even a beautiful, heavy, well-armed stag in the prime of life is no match for a vehicle. Every October on Exmoor there are road accidents involving stags, as they chase up and down the countryside left, right and all ways, and jump out into the road without a thought. A big stag smashing into a car makes a serious collision, and many times over the years I've had a phone call asking me to go and help finish off a deer that has been knocked down and had its legs broken. Autumn is when drivers need to go most carefully on the winding roads of the countryside, and pay attention to the road signs which warn of deer. They're there for a reason.

Once I was driving down the road below Stoke Pero church when a big stag walked out into the road right in front of me. He was going up the valley onto the moors, being pushed out of the territory by what must have been an even bigger stag. I managed to stop the truck, jump out, get the camera, set it up and film him before he disappeared into the woods. He was so distracted that he didn't even notice me.

JONATHAN HAWES

Stags will fight viciously during the rut

Hind and her yearling, Rackenford

A big autumn stag crossing the road at Stoke Pero during the rutting season

Out stalking with the village lads

The hinds stay in groups during the rutting season, constantly on the look-out for danger. In the autumn, when the calves have grown into yearlings, they still live with their mothers in groups together. The hinds are very protective, which makes stalking them tricky. If a hind thinks she's heard something unusual, she'll give out a loud bark which warns all the deer in the valley that something's wrong. Although she does it to protect her calf or yearling, the whole herd will take notice. Sometimes, very rarely, a young stag will bark too.

Over the years I've taught myself how to stalk the animals, and learnt their signals. Though I've been doing it for more than four decades, I'm still learning. With wildlife, you never stop; and I like taking other people out stalking too, and sharing what I know.

To stalk the Exmoor red deer, you need the right clothing – camouflage gear in the summer, and something rusty coloured in the autumn, and a mask. After that, the most important thing is to look into the sky. See which way the clouds are going, and that gives you an idea which way the wind is blowing. The wind must be blowing towards you, away from the deer. Often on Exmoor the wind whirls around in the valleys, so you have to be careful, and circle round if you need to. Once the wind's right you can get down on your knees and start crawling. You move forward slowly when the deer are busy, or when they're lying down having a bit of a sleep

Stalking during the rutting season near Willingford Bridge

A good shot of a beautiful stag near Willingford Bridge

This big stag got a little too close for comfort

after a night stealing the farmers' crops. They especially like cobs of corn, and they love to carry them about. I often see the cobs scattered around on the farmer's land.

You have to be very, very quiet. Deer have very keen hearing as well as sight, so if you so much as snap a stick they'll know something's wrong. Usually at the bottom of valleys there's a stream, which can be a help – you can get in the water, and although you end up soaked, the sound of the water covers your steps.

No matter how quiet you are, as you approach they'll sense that you're there at some point, and they'll throw their heads up and watch for you, first once and then again. That's when you have to stay still, until they've relaxed again and you have the chance to get behind some cover – a clump of ferns will do – to set up your camera. I always film freehand, so as not to worry about a tripod; some people use a monopod. Once you're behind the camera, the stag will stare straight at you – but he won't recognise you. You must look him out, and then you know you've got him on camera. Patience is what you need, and you've got to stay completely still even if a stag comes very close. It can be very frightening.

Each stag is different. There's one special animal that I've followed for four years. I can always tell him by his voice; he's dark-coloured and dark-horned, and big, with four points on the top of each antler and a three-

The stag stared: he looked dangerous

They stopped and looked back

foot-wide spread across his antlers. I usually find him somewhere near Dunkery Beacon, or in the valleys round Stoke Pero. He'll normally round up between 20 and 30 hinds, and take them off to the woods. It's a challenge to film any deer then, because they're so easily lost. So I'll go into the wood before dawn, when it's still dark, and let the daylight come to me — and then the stags often come as well. I'll be wearing a full mask, and lying down and waiting very quietly, behind a tree with the camera ready. If I'm properly hidden the stags will approach, sometimes to within ten yards. I do take big chances, but that's the challenge — and that's when I get good results.

One rutting season near Willingford Bridge, up on the open moor, I filmed a fine stag with all his rights, three and two, a beautiful young animal near the prime of his life. I was less than 15 paces away from him by the end, and there was so little cover that I was having to hide behind some gorse bushes. The day was not far from darkness, when suddenly he stared straight at me. If you're on an open common and a stag in the rut notices you, you must stay put, but I always try to have a tree nearby just in case he attacks.

That evening there was no tree, so I had no choice — I just had to stare him out. He stuck his chest out and turned to go, and then suddenly he stopped and gave me an evil look with a glad, rolling eye, and I wondered which way to go if the worst came to the worst and I needed to run. I knew that really I didn't have any choice, though — I could never out run an angry stag.

For a moment I was really frightened; but then the stag decided that he wasn't interested in me. With a shake of his pointed antlers he turned away and began to run, when out of nowhere another big stag joined him. They ran together, one chasing the other, for a little way as evening fell; and just when I thought I'd lost them both, they suddenly stopped and both looked back at me. It was a fantastic moment, before they tossed their heads and ran on out of sight.

On 1 October the stag-hunting season begins on Exmoor. There are three main packs, the Devon and Somerset, the Tiverton, and the Quantock staghounds. Most people on Exmoor are hunting people, and that's how they get their living, from the farriers and pony girls to the stable boys and dog handlers.

WESTERN DAILY PRESS

The start of the hunting season is a big event. With thousands of people arriving from up country for the stag-hunting season, and the hunt balls and other social events, the whole area feels the difference, from the farmhouse bed-and-breakfasts to the shops. The farmers and landowners of Exmoor tolerate and protect the deer mostly for the sake of hunting; and if hunting stopped, so many people say they'll destroy the deer that I don't think it would be long before there were none left. If that was to happen it would be a very sad day.

As a film-maker I love Exmoor and the deer. I lie down flat on my face for hours and wait for them to come out and show me what they do. You have to crawl and be prepared to get wet, and it's not always comfortable; but it's worth it. Some stags are real characters, and I get to know them over the years. Some even become famous, and gain such a name for themselves that many people remember them long after they've gone.

Bruno, the king of Rackenford in the early Nineties, was one of the most well-known stags in the area in his time. People used to come from miles around to see him. Normally he wasn't afraid of them, and he

Bruno, the Rackenford stag

used to go on the lawn at Worthy Folly House at Rackenford Manor, where Dick and Simone Williams lived, without any fear, even if the dogs were barking. They often let him into their garden and kept watch over him. If he scented the hunt, though, he was off straight away to make his escape; and for many years he managed it, until in the end even the Tiverton Staghounds gave him special protection.

Bruno always kept a fine group of hinds, and for years he beat off all challengers, including his own son, in time. It was a fight I managed to film; it lasted a full six minutes, and you could hear the clash of antlers all round the valley.

I filmed Bruno for seven years. He was something special to me, my own challenge, a symbol of the perfect stag – strong, heavy, with a deep roar and huge antlers. I used to wait until the end of September to see him, and I'd follow him, filming, until the end of November. He chased me many times, and twice I've been up a tree and frightened to come down when Bruno was down below.

In the end, though, his very beauty and power brought him down. A trophy-hunter shot him, someone who was never caught. Bruno was the king of the forest; but they found him dead in a valley near Witheridge.

People in Devon love the sound of the roaring stags. If you go into South Molton in the rutting season many people will be talking about what they've heard, and where. A favourite place to listen to the roaring is Drayton Rails at Marsh Bridge, where all through the rutting season you'll find vehicles parked as people stop to listen. The deeper and stronger the roar, the older and bigger the stag.

It's a strange, haunting sound, and it can be quite frightening to hear. Every year during the rutting season we'll make soup and sandwiches, and late in the evening, once it's dark, we'll go out as a family, Julie, me, our granddaughters Roxy and Louise and our friends Mike and Jill, to hear the stags roar. Even at 10 o'clock at night they'll still be throwing their challenge across the valleys to each other.

If you can send out a roar in the right way yourself during the rut, you can call the stags to you – though the people who do this always make sure they have a vehicle nearby, to take cover in. Our friend Paul can do it brilliantly. One night he was so successful that he called a stag as well as a whole herd of very interested cows, which came hurrying across the field towards us all of a sudden, so quickly that they were rattling the trees. We all jumped in the car very fast that time.

A stag's roar is a special signal which other stags understand, and it's how he finds his challenger, of about the same size and weight as himself. One of the things I most enjoy is coming out very early in the morning, half past four or earlier, while it's still dark. I listen to the roaring to find out where the stags are, and then go towards them, getting on the other side of the wind and into position ready to film them as the sun rises. It's something I usually do alone. No-one will come in with me: they're too frightened. But to me, filming the stags roaring at the start of the new day is a challenge. If I can catch a stag close up, it's just brilliant – the trembles go right through my body. And if it's a stag I know already, it's even better.

One year I met the fine Poldhouse Combe stag again during the rut that I'd seen in velvet earlier the same year. He was a strong beast, and I followed him right through the rut. Underneath Anstey Stone he kept a herd of over 30 hinds, and he rutted right through Cloggs Valley that year.

Poldhouse Combe stag roaring at Cloggs Valley

A big stag, with all his rights and four a-top, roaring at Badgercombe

A big stag with his party of hinds, rubbing his antlers on a tree at Stoke Pero

One of the best stags on Exmoor was in Badgercombe valley, an animal with all his rights and four points on the top of each antler, and the biggest body anyone had seen in a long time. I filmed him throwing his challenge to another stag that he'd met and fought the week before, and I could see a clump of grass on his antlers where he'd dug them in the ground a moment before in his rage. He had 30 or 40 hinds, and he kept them for four or five weeks. For Exmoor people, a stag like this in the rut is an important symbol of the power and wildness of the animals.

The roaring of stags, and their challenges and fights, are beautiful and exciting to see. But the deer also have their own secrets, which are less obvious.

One of the ways that stags mark territory is by rubbing their antlers on a tree to leave their scent on it. Once during the rutting season I went into Stoke Pero, out below Dunkery Beacon in the heart of Exmoor, and got down to the woods in the river valley below Stoke Pero church, which are well-known for their deer. It was pitch black as I parked the truck. I stopped and listened to the stags roaring to get my bearings, and made sure the wind was right; then I climbed up a steep bank into the woods.

There was a big tree lying across the track there, so I lay down next to it, hoping that the stags I could hear roaring would come my way. It was only when daylight came, half an hour later, that I realised I was lying right across the main deer track through the woods. There was nothing I could do but keep still as a big stag came along with his hinds, so close that he was just a few yards away, and I watched as he stopped and rubbed his antlers against a tree to mark the place.

As he went by there was more roaring behind him, and out came five or six big stags, one so big his antlers were three feet apart. They stepped all the way round me, walking right past where I was lying on the front of my face, completely still. I didn't dare to move.

But I must have made a noise; because suddenly one of them

In Stoke Pero wood, one stag stopped and looked straight into my eyes

stopped, and he looked through the trees straight into my eyes. At that moment I didn't know what to do. If he'd decided to come at me, I wouldn't have stood a chance, he was so close. I stayed completely still, and in the end he walked on. I have to admit, I shouldn't go doing things like that. I was shaking with fear.

Another way of scenting the ground to warn other stags to stay away is wallowing. All deer like to wallow in mud, to get rid of the ticks and other insects in their coats. Not many people see this side of the deers' lives, how they keep themselves healthy and clean and how they use the earth they live on.

A wallow is very important for deer, and when they find the right kind of place they'll come back to it for years and years. It needs to be somewhere with a small continuous spring, which spreads out over the ground, making the whole area a bit boggy. The deer will work up the boggy ground with their feet, rolling and bathing in the mud, and keeping the area a foot or more deep in slurry, mud and water.

During one rutting season I went to film the deer at a very old and well-used wallow under three oak trees. Day after day for five days I took my camera and climbed up the tree, but although the water was muddy, meaning that the deer had visited recently, I never caught sight of any animals. I knew that something was going wrong, and in the end I decided that I must be arriving at the wrong time of day.

So the next day I got there very early in the morning, when it was still completely dark. Carrying my lunch and my camera, I quietly climbed up the tree again, settling down on a big branch in camouflage gear and leaning my body against the tree trunk so that it looked like part of the trunk itself. Then I kept very still.

When dawn came I saw that I'd been right, as I saw the deer, stepping down through the trees in the early light to wallow, a little yearling and then a calf, covered in spots. It rolled in the mud, climbed out and shook itself. ten or 11 hinds followed, and then finally down came a lovely royal stag and lay down in the muddy water. An amazing feeling went through me as I sat and filmed that fantastic moment.

I shall never forget what happened next. As the stag got out he shook himself, and then he looked straight into the tree where I was sitting; and the next second he was running so fast out of the wallow that all the hinds standing around just stared at him.

Deer in wallow

What had happened was that although I was well camouflaged, I'd forgotten to hide the little red light on the front of the camera which blinks every time you film. The stag had suddenly seen it, and had been startled into running away. But I kept very still, and before long he came back. It was the middle of the rutting season, and he was more interested in his hinds than in strange little red lights in the trees.

As the month turns from September to October, up on the moors the air becomes chilly even in the daytime, and all the mountain ash trees are loaded with red berries. Even if there's bad weather ahead, the moor provides plenty of food for the blackbird and thrush when the winter comes. By the time the rutting season is over, from early November onwards, most of the leaves are off the trees, the stags and hinds come back all friendly again. The stags all begin to group together, to travel back to their home ground. They're only enemies during the rut, and all that's forgotten now. You see them moving across the fields and through the trees and combes as they make their way back to their home territories, to meet the other stags and join in their home herds again. A stag will travel 20 miles during the rut, always coming to the same place; so some of them have a long way to go. This is a good time to film them as well, as they travel the deer tracks right across Exmoor.

Looking up the Barle Valley towards Tarr Steps and beyond to Winsford Hill is like

Royal stag eating hawthorn berries, Twitchen

looking through a tunnel from moorland to farmland. This is where the red deer travel, and the ravens, buzzards and hawks live above, in the big oak trees and silver birches.

After the rut the big stags go away and lie down. It's very urgent for them to put on weight now, after not eating for so long; so they start looking for better keep, especially the farmer's crops, and will eat berries and leaves and bracken too. Hawthorn berries are their favourites, and they'll nibble the berries from the lower branches of the

Autumn near Hawkridge

Looking down the Barle valley

View from Winsford Hill with fog in the valleys

thorn trees while the fieldfares in their hundreds onto the berries higher up. On Winsford Hill, down towards the village of Exford, there are hawthorn berries on every thorn tree. This is where the fieldfare flocks and the redwing feed, and all the leaves turn their colour as they fall to the ground. In some ways nature is very generous; but it can also be rough. Every year some animals are so worn out by the rutting season that their journey home is very hard.

As autumn moves on the colours change day by day. The rose bay willow herb dies down, and the trees turn to every shade of gold and brown and red. You find sweet chestnuts under the chestnut trees at this time of year, and I always peel and try one first, for bitterness, then when I've found the right tree I bring them home and bake them, or eat them raw.

Hundreds of times I've bent down and drunk from the edge of a river, too, especially high up on the moors, where the water runs clear. You do get dead sheep in the water sometimes, but it's never affected me. On Exmoor we say that the water passing over the stones purifies it. I don't know if that's true, but I know I've never been harmed, by drinking it.

Autumn is the time for cider, my favourite drink at a traditional farm. In my younger days, my friend Mr Clements had a cider press at his farm, a big, heavy metal plate with a

Near Five Cross Ways on the way to Hawkridge

Moorland off Dunkery

Exmoor pony on Anstey Common

screw running up the middle and a big box beneath; and in the autumn he'd set it to work. He'd start by going out into his orchards and bagging up the windfalls, leaving them outside for a while. The deer would often come out of the woods and tip the bags over. They liked the taste of cider apples too.

Gangs of us used to go shooting at Mr Clements' farm, and afterwards we'd have buns and bread, home-baked by his wife and daughter, in the old farmhouse, and a big mug of tea. I've watched Mr Clements make cider. He'd make it properly, with a lot of bite, out of his sacks of rotten apples. He'd put a layer of apples into the press, followed by a layer of straw, and continue in that way, layering up all the apples until the press was full. Then he'd twist the handle on the big screw to press the plate hard down on the apples and straw, and a trickle of juice would come out of the bottom of the press. Every so many days he'd turn the handle on the press and squeeze a little more, and gradually there'd be enough juice to put into big jugs and leave to settle and brew until the winter. He made really rough cider that way, good drink with a real edge, yellow and cloudy, not like today's mass-produced clear drink. An evening drinking Mr Clements' cider would send you to sleep nicely.

Out stalking in the autumn, I pick hazelnuts along the hedges in the misty mornings, when the ground's frosty and crisp near the river, and my feet crunch on the frozen grass. The leaves hang still and gold along the valleys. It'll just take a little wind now, and down they'll come.

For most of the year the Exmoor ponies run wild on the moor; but they all belong to someone, and every October they're rounded up near Landacre Bridge, when the foals are old enough to be parted from their mothers. It's a pretty sight, with the animals all together after the summer's grazing up on the moorland. The best foals are always picked out to be returned to the moor to carry on and breed again, which keeps the herd strong and healthy; and the rest are taken away from their mothers, branded to say that they're pure-bred Exmoors, and sold.

The roundup isn't easy. The ponies are wild animals, and it takes skill and tact to bring them all in and keep them calm. The Exmoor Pony Society usually helps the local farmers with the roundup of horses.

The ponies lead their own lives, watched by very few and tamed and ridden by hardly anyone. The stallions challenge each other for the mares, the mares give birth, and the foals grow, all undisturbed by people. But the farmers maintain them and watch over them, and the herd is in good condition because of their care. The Dartmoor ponies are shaggier than the Exmoor, and they're all different colours: black, white, gingery. Our Exmoor ponies aren't as mixed in colour as the Dartmoor ones – they're lighter, with a lovely mane. When the ferns change colour for winter, they turn the same rusty brown colour as the ponies.

Cock pheasant

As the days grow shorter and colder, many of Exmoor's animals take a rest. The hedgehogs curl up in dry leaves and sleep for the winter; toads, cold and clammy, hide in damp places. In October and November the badgers start getting sleepy, and start to spend most of their time underground. Through the summer months they've fed heavily, and laid down fat to survive the winter; and by the time autumn comes, things are going quiet. At the end of September the badgers clean out their setts, throwing out their old bedding and taking in fresh grass; and that's when you know it's the mating season. The little cubs will be born deep underground in January.

Autumn also brings the pheasant shooting season. There are two main shoots, at Molland and Filleigh, and people from all over Britain, and as far afield as France and Germany, pay tremendous money to enjoy the sport.

You see pheasants everywhere on Exmoor, waddling about wearing their bright autumn colours; but it's unusual to find one with a character of its own. Once I was digging a grave in the village of Charles, near Brayford, when a pheasant came down and wouldn't leave me alone. He kept jumping on top of the shovel when I was heaving stones out, and attacking my clothes with his spurs, and he stayed with me until I'd finished the grave.

This pheasant had decided he liked people, and he would do the same to anyone who came into the churchyard. When there was a funeral he'd follow the coffin up to the doorway of the church, catch hold of the vicar's black cloak and hang on. It was all many people could do to stop laughing, even at such a solemn moment. But his interest in humans didn't do him much good in the end. He was run over by a car right outside the church.

As November comes in we often get the first snow, just a skitter, not much; and on the moors it can be very, very cold. This is the time to look for the golden plover and the snipe, which always come before the cold weather. There are pigeons and woodcocks in the hedges; fieldfares flock, and the chaffinches gather under the beech trees in their hundreds to feed on the fallen beech mast there; and up on Winsford Hill you might see a yellowhammer singing on top of a hawthorn tree.

Autumn is the time to start feeding the birds in the garden with clean peanuts or a good mixed grain. All summer the birds have fed themselves on insects, worms, berries and seeds, but they suffer in the cold weather, and many die. Putting food out in the garden helps the little birds through the hard times.

The raven is the biggest black bird on Exmoor, the largest of the crow family, with a four-inch beak. It's also the earliest bird to look for a mate. In November you might be lucky and see two ravens mating high in the sky,

Blue tits feeding

diving up and down over combe or common as they play. They're already thinking of spring.

By the end of the summer months, the fox cubs that were born last spring have grown up. They don't play with spiders and beetles now: as the white tip on their tails develops, they begin to hunt properly for themselves. Often all they're thinking about is taking the pheasant poults, which upsets the keeper, who has to go out and shoot the foxes in his turn. When the autumn starts to chill the air and the bracken turns the colour of the foxes' coats, the grown-up cubs leave their mother and go their own way, ready to face the cold weather to come alone. The vixen rests, hiding in her den and hunting now only for herself. It will be winter before her mating season starts.

October is when the salmon start running, as they come up to spawn in the gin-clear, cold waters that rise at the top of the moors and fill the brimming pools and shallow river beds of the Exmoor rivers where they rise, the Exe, the Barle and the Bray. Each year the fish return to Exmoor in pairs, hundreds of them, to the same spawning beds. They've made a journey of hundreds of miles in from the Atlantic, and it's fantastic to watch their energy as they jump the weirs. My father could catch salmon on the move, standing at the waterside and gaffing them as they swam. A gaff is a specially made tool for catching fish, a crook with a barb attached to it. Sometimes we caught some nice fish for the pot that way.

Thirty years ago, when I'd just moved to Bishops Nympton, I was involved with some people who were out to catch the salmon. One Sunday afternoon one of them caught a huge salmon in the Bray river, just down from the village. It weighed 27 pounds, and its head alone, when we cut it off, weighed six and a half pounds. Its eyes were as big as old pennies, and when we cut it up the cutlets were so wide that one alone could scarcely fit in the frying-pan. You shouldn't do these things nowadays, though – you'd be breaking the law if you did.

These days many people arrive on Exmoor when the salmon fishing season opens, and stay in the big hotels to fish along the Lyn, Mowl and Taw rivers. It's all strictly controlled by licence, and it's an expensive pastime. But to me, filming the salmon is a bigger challenge still.

Every year I try to film them coming up the Barle river to spawn in the stickles, the safe, shallow places high up on the moors where the water is clear. The fish make the long journey up the Barle towards Landacre by the end of October and early November. On really frosty mornings in November when the trees are bare, you might see them at Withypool, or on the weirs, a streak of silver and pink and a dark shape swiftly moving through the running water.

There are three types of salmon in the Exmoor waters: the silverback, the red and the greenback. The greenback is the smallest of the three, with the red the most common. The salmon need the heavy rains of late autumn to make the journey upstream, through all the weirs on the rivers. If the weather has been fine they'll wait downstream until the rain begins to fall in torrents, non-stop, and when the water's bank-high in the rivers they begin to move, to get to the safer places high on the stickles. Some will get trapped on the grass on the way up; but very few lose their way.

The salmon run together in pairs, the male, or keeper fish, with a hook on his

RICHARD TAYLOR-JONES

Sow salmon jumping a weir

RICHARD TAYLOR-JONES

The cock salmon, or keeper fish, fights his way upstream

*Barle valley in autumn,
near Marsh Bridge*

upper lip, with the female, the sow. When they reach the stickles, they find a calm, very shallow place in the clear, cold water where it runs over the little stones and shingle. They pick a place to work, or make a fish nest, in the shingle of the river bottom, near the bank. If there are quite a few pairs of salmon, they'll make a line of works right across the river.

The pairs of fish will lie on their stomachs and shunt their bodies along. Using their tails like shovels, they'll dig a small, shallow pit, like a basin, on the river bed. Then the keeper and the sow lie side by side in the hollow.

First the female lays her eggs, and then the cock fish will fertilise them. They'll spend the next two or three days playing together like this, until all their eggs are laid and fertilised, and they're spent. Then both fish go to the front of the pit, dig another pit there, and with very fine sand or shingle they cover over their eggs. When the eggs are completely covered, the fish will select three or four big stones, lift them with their tails, and place them on top of the work. That's how you can tell that they've been there and they've finished. And then they begin making their way downstream again, drifting slowly back towards the sea.

Many never make it. In recent years I've seen a lot of salmon get a diseased kind of fungus, white spots, which weakens them and makes them very sick. They've been coming in from the ocean covered in sea lice, which take a while to drop off in the fresh water; and then they seem to catch the fungus. They might make it to spawn, but they don't get back to the sea – they all die. Something about this new illness in the salmon reminds me of myxomatosis years ago, when all the rabbits were wiped out. It's terrible to see them dying.

High above the valleys, where the water runs small on the moors, you might be lucky and see otters in the autumn. One of the most well-respected farriers on Exmoor lives by Sheldon Water, up a long valley. It's a very lonesome, quiet place, and they do see otters there from time to time.

A farrier has to travel all round the countryside visiting farms, stables and studs to shoe the horses for working, hunting, trekking, point-to-point and steeplechasing. All horses need shoes, and fitting them properly is a skilled job. Many's the time I've enjoyed watching the farrier at work, how he trims the horse's foot with a big knife, bows the shoe, sizes it, warms it up and presses it to the hoof. You see the smoke rising from the hoof, and there's a burning smell, but the horse stands calmly – it doesn't hurt him. When the shoe's bedded in he nails it on, knocking the nails up into the hoof at an angle until they come up through it; then he snips the ends off with a pair of pliers and tucks it in neat and tidy.

There was a time when the otters were nearly extinct here, but they're coming

Sheldon Water, a tributary of the Barle River, where otters are sometimes seen

back to Exmoor now. Most people don't realise that they've got so far upstream, though. Once a farmer rang me to say that he'd just spotted an otter at his fishpond, taking his carp, and would I like to come and film it? I went straight away, but it was too late: the otter had gone, though the farmer watched it for a full 15 minutes. He was a lucky man to see that. But mostly it's the night fishermen who have the best chance of seeing them, in the spring of the year when the sea trout are running. Though even then, it's just a quiet splash by moonlight, and the otter's gone. They don't stay around.

Not everyone is very happy about the otters. They blame them for the fish that are disappearing from fish-ponds. They don't even think about the mink, though, which run wild on Exmoor too, where they've escaped from farms, and which also like a bit of fish, especially well-fed carp.

The rivers of the moor are always an attraction, for people as well as wildlife. Years ago I took Julie and two other friends over the moors for an outing on a Sunday afternoon. We'd had torrents and torrents of rain, and when we got down as far as the ford across the river at Tarr Steps we saw that the water was running very high. Plenty of cars had turned back instead of driving across the ford; but I thought I knew my river, and I decided to give it a go.

All was well until we'd got three parts across, when all of a sudden the van started to sail, and we were swept right into the steps themselves with a crash. The high water started pouring into the van, which was rocking and bumping against the bridge. I tried to prise the door open and shouted to my pregnant wife, 'Get in the back!' The water was building up and I couldn't open the door, so I put my feet up on the dashboard and carried on pushing.

Outside on the steps there were lots of people watching, and as the waters rose inside the van they all started gathering on the bridge with their cameras, taking photos of our desperate situation. I couldn't believe it. I wound the window down.

'Look, get in the water and help us, you silly sods, instead of taking photos,' I shouted. 'Or we shall drown!' When they understood the real danger we were in, everybody piled into the river, and between them they managed to push us out to safety. It was a frightening experience, and it taught me a lesson. You should always respect wild river waters, no matter how easy and gentle they seem.

In November, when heavy rains often swell the rivers and the leaves have mostly fallen, the roe deer loses his antlers. They're small, nothing like as big as those of the red deer, and they're dainty and hard to find, in the valley woodlands, near trees with damage to the trunk about a foot off the ground. In November the little deers' heads itch just as the red deer's do, and they scratch them in the same way, on any tree they can find, until their antlers drop off.

If someone sees a roe deer it's a rare event, and usually they're gone in a flash. My sister Thelma was recently thrilled to see three of them, their white tails bobbing as they bounced away.

It's very rare to find a pair of roe antlers: I've only managed it once in my whole life. To drop both antlers near to each other, the buck has to be living in an undisturbed place; and since they're nervous little animals, and always running away, this doesn't happen very often. Unlike the red deers' antlers, which change according to the age of the animal, the roe deers' mostly look alike: small, around a foot in height, with just two points on the top.

As autumn closes in on the moor, there are weeks of heavy rain and mist. This is the best time of year to see the weird, strangely coloured fungi that spring up all round the moor, especially at North Hill, near Minehead. There are clear, crisp days, and days of fog, when it's silent, grey and overcast, with the sun breaking through, and if you go up and look down the valleys, all you'll see are the tips of the trees poking out of the white mist. The moods of the moor are always changing, and as the cold weather sets in, Nature closes down and gets ready for the hard winter ahead.

JONATHAN HAWES

WESTERN DAILY PRESS

WINTER

Winter on Exmoor can be harsh, with deep snow, bitter cold and frost and thick ice. With the visitors gone, and the cream teas closed up for the winter, the season brings wild, empty days in the moor, glittering with frost or overtaken with rain and mist, when the sun seems to have gone for good and the trees stand black and empty against the sky. It's the season when the owl flies, gliding silently as it hunts through the night, or sitting in a tree giving out its lonely cry; and down in the villages it's the time of parties, whist drives and fundraising, warm firesides and good drinking.

In years gone by, when I was a child, we always used to keep a couple of pigs, and the start of winter was the time of slaughter. The pigs were very important to us: that was how the family got through until the following spring. First one pig was killed, and then the other three months later; but the work of taking care of them carried on all the year round. They lived in a shed not far from the house which was always infested with rats, who would come to eat the pigs' food and lived under their troughs. From time to time my dad would get me to come out to the pig-shed with him and lift up the end of the trough. As I lifted it, the big brown rats would come running out from underneath. My dad stood and caught each one with his fists as it ran up the doorframe. He never missed, and as he banged each rat it would drop down dead on the floor.

At the end of November a slaughterman arrived to help Dad kill the first pig. The pig wasn't stupid: it knew very well what was going to happen, and as they slung it up by the back legs it would start to scream. I didn't like the screaming, but in the end I had to get used to it. That was how life was.

When the slaughtering was over, we hung the pig's carcass up in the slee, an open shed behind the house, on a hook above where the mangle and the washing tub stood. Then the hard work began. My job was to scald the pig with hot water out of a funnel, and rub the bristles off it. Every single bit of it was carefully cleaned. We salted down the cuts of meat in big round red pottery bowls, which you had to leave to stand in the cold store; there weren't any fridges then, so that was how you preserved the meat. We made hogs' puddings, tripe out of the stomach, brawn out of the head and sausages out of the innards. At the end of it all, I used to get the pig's bladder for a football. We never wasted anything. It was a very hard way of living, though we didn't complain. The pork was delicious; and not everyone could afford to rear two pigs a year.

In the weeks before Christmas we'd have the salt pork ready, and we'd kill a goose or two as well, and at Christmas itself we'd each hang up an old sock for Father Christmas who'd be coming down the chimney. We all believed in Father Christmas then, and we were pleased with what he'd leave us in our stockings – a big orange, a doll or a teddy, and some jokey things like a lump of coal.

I remember snow-white Christmases from my boyhood. The weather was colder then, and there'd be snowdrifts halfway up the sides of the telegraph poles sometimes. The roads would be full right up, and we'd have to turn out and shovel the snow, taking out big blocks of it just to get through.

We always had a Christmas tree, and every year my dad and I used to walk two miles to a special holly tree we knew, to cut holly with berries for the house. Holly was very important. We had no fancy trimmings then, but with six children in the family we used to make our own out of paper, sticking strips in big loops and chains and painting the paper ourselves.

We used to pray for snow, and if it came we played out on home-made wooden sledges or, if we didn't have wood, we'd use a piece of galvanised tin to slide on, seven or eight of us at a time. Once someone nearly lost his fingers when we were sledging in the dark and he caught them on the edge. A tin sledge like that would go like a rocket with all of us sitting on it.

Christmas Day was a holiday. For dinner my mum would cook the goose, and my dad always used to have a big piece of pork with crackling. My uncles, Tony,

Sunset on the moor

Arthur and Bill, used to come to our house, and after dinner they'd play cards or games with a spinning top. But on Christmas morning I was in church with the choir, walking at the head of the choirboys, all dressed up in my proper gear with a frilly collar round my neck. After Christmas church we'd go down to the vicarage, and if we'd been good through the year the vicar would give us a book with our name written inside. All these years later, I've still got the Christmas books I was given then, Robinson Crusoe, Dick Barton, and others. And I still remember how pleased and proud I felt.

Winter had its share of sorrows as well. In 1985 I was working part-time on Herbert Thorne's farm, and one freezing morning I arrived very early. It was a day of fierce frost, and the gorse on the rough ground looked bare and dead.

I loaded up the tractor with hay to feed the animals as usual, but as soon as I started driving it down through the field, a big brown object underneath a thorn tree caught my eye. I thought it was a deer resting at first, until a little dog came away from it and started running towards me, and I saw that the dark shape was a man. Herbert had had a heart attack the evening before, and had frozen stiff where he'd fallen down and died at the edge of the field. His little dog, Flash, was only a collie pup; but she'd stayed with him all night, lying underneath his arm and keeping watch.

This is when sheep feel the cold

It hurt me a lot to find such a good man frozen in the bitter cold. He'd been a friend to me, and a kind person. Years before, I used to like helping Herbert when he was busy with the spring lambing season. There were always lambs to rear by hand and feed from bottles in the farmhouse. One year we had 16 orphan lambs, so one day after work I took four of them home to Bishops Nympton with me.

Julie was used to my arriving home with all sorts of creatures, but even she'd been a bit surprised at the four lambs. We made them a little pen in the back garden, and when they grew up one of them turned out to be a ram; the rest were ewes. They used to like running up and down the next-door neighbour's steps, and Sheila, the neighbour, didn't mind a bit. Sandy, my lurcher dog, used to love playing with Blackie, the big black ram, and it always made us laugh to watch them, Sandy barking and Blackie head-butting him back, each creature arguing in its own way. We never sheared our sheep, or had them slaughtered. They were part of the family, and when they grew too big for our garden I took them to a smallholding in South Molton, where I did odd jobs to help with their keep.

All this was in my mind that bitter winter morning as I went to the water pump to get water to the cows, and got on with feeding the animals as the ambulance arrived. Herbert died on 29 January 1985, the coldest night of the year, and when the time came for his funeral I was the one to dig his grave. It was a very hard task to lay him into the earth at Twitchen church, in the same grave as his beloved wife, who had died some years before. I buried him right underneath some high trees, where there's a rookery with the birds coming and going all year long. I couldn't help thinking that it would be a good place for him to rest. There's no better sound than the calling of the birds in the trees.

After Herbert died, one of the things I had to do on the farm was to drown five black kittens that had just been born. Nobody likes drowning kittens, and when I got to the last one, instead of holding her down in the water I slipped her into my pocket and took her home instead. We called her Smokey, and she grew up into a nice, kind cat with fluffy black fur and dainty white socks who became a lovely family pet and lived to be nearly 20 years old. She never took a bird in her life, even though our garden is always full of nesting boxes and bird feeders. I was always glad she was there. Every day for twenty years Smokey the farm cat reminded me of Herbert, one of the kindest bosses I'd known.

In the winter months, when fierce frosts leave the moors bitterly cold, and the

Rookery at Twitchen Church

colour seems to have gone away from the moors for all time, the red deer drop down into the shelter of the valleys and live among the trees. The rutting season has ended now, and the stags are poor and thin, their bodies pinched and tucked up. They're very hungry after all their efforts in the autumn, and have to build themselves up again. So their biggest need now is for good grazing, at a time of year when there are no leaves and little grass. The farmer's fields have never looked so inviting.

On fine winter days people will take advantage of the lovely weather and walk up on the moors; and the deer will do the same. 'There were 32 stags up there, Johnny,' my friend Steve told me one winter, 'and the biggest one was a six-and four-top.'

But the farmer Tony Thorne had a different view. 'Twasn't 32, 'twas 33, Johnny,' he said when I saw him going to the hide. 'I know. I saw them eating my swedes.'

Exmoor ponies on Molland Moor

The deer do eat swedes, and a big herd can ruin a whole crop in one night. Despite this, many farmers like to see them, and some, like Tony, will leave a corner of the crop especially for them.

Some deer will find their own ways of getting the food they need. My friend Tim tells of a hind he knows in North Molton with two calves. 'She goes into a cover where they feed the pheasant poults, shakes the big tin drum with her forehead between her eyes, and gets the pellets out, Johnny,' he tells me. The pheasant poults are fed on pellets in big drums among the oak trees when they're small, and when they're bigger they're fed on wheat. You'll sometimes hear a stag rub his antlers against the wheat drums to get the grain out; but I've never known a hind go one better and take the pellets. But Tim is sure. 'It's what she does, Johnny,' he says. 'She doesn't wait for the wheat – she gets the pellets out first.' He laughs. 'You can see why her calves are so good-looking every year.'

In the winter the stags are all friendly again, and they herd together so peacefully to feed and roam that it's hard to believe they were such enemies only 12 weeks before. At this time of year some herds contain over 50 deer, hinds and their yearlings, with a few stags; others are stags alone. Sometimes they settle in one spot for weeks at a time, until the local farmer moves them on. It can do them good to mix them up a bit, and stop them interbreeding. But most of all, in the winter months the hinds are pregnant, and the stags are tired; and both spend the time quietly, feeding and resting.

While the deer are in the valleys, the ponies are up on the cold moors. Everyone loves to see the Exmoor ponies with their shaggy winter coats and their thick manes. They don't mind the winter cold – they eat the dry bracken and rough gorse, and it does no harm to them. Even in January, when it's misty and raining, when the ground is slippery and you can't see more than 50 yards ahead of you, or when it's icy and freezing, they live happily enough on the wide open moor, turning their backs on the cold and waiting patiently for the spring.

Winter means work of a different kind for me. It was Boxing Day 2001 when I took my two sons and three mates to begin work on building the new badger house near Twitchen. Two inches of snow had fallen, and we were late starting, it being Christmas and relaxed. So it wasn't until 10 o'clock that I drove our truck across the steep fields down to the valley.

It's a remote spot, high up on the moors near Cussacombe Post. Tony, the farmer, had been working with big machines on his swede crop, and I drove across gullies of mud three and a half feet wide to get down to the bottom of the field.

I had a 21-foot new scaffolding tower to put up, on a base of railway sleepers and tied down by guy ropes, and my sons Craig and Stuart started building the room for the hide itself, 6 foot by 4 foot, at the top of the tower, where in the coming months it would sway among the birch-tree tops when a high wind blew, but would remain stable. Later there would be another room below, at ground level, with a connecting trapdoor and ladder between the two, and a verandah with windows at the front of the top room, to give me more options for filming. The work that day should have taken us a couple of hours and then I was going to take everyone for a pint.

But nothing went right. While I was filming the area the others started work on the scaffolding tower. Maybe it was the Christmas dinner and all the Christmas spirits the day before, but it wasn't until one and a half hours later that someone noticed that they'd built it upside down, and they had to start again. Meanwhile fixing the boards to the tower wasn't going well either.

We carried on. Hours passed, the sun came out, it started to get very windy and then snow began to fall. It was three o'clock before we piled into the truck, and began to climb up the field across the muddy gullies.

We were three parts up the hill when the truck started sliding down again backwards. Everyone bailed out and I was left steering as it slid right back to the bottom of the valley, 20 yards below. It was a nasty moment, and a wonder I didn't finish down in the woods. Three hours later we were still there. We were glad to see Tony Thorne come over with his tractor and grateful to him when he pulled the truck right up and over the hill in the dark.

Tony is a very kind man, and loves wildlife. When he first took me to see the sett, where the year before the Ministry man had culled the badgers, we weren't sure if anything was still living there.

The holes looked dead, the field deserted. But that didn't mean there were no badgers. It wasn't long before Tony spotted one black and white hair caught on a barbed-wire fence, low down by the ground. 'That's the badger's path,' I said, bending down to look. 'And do you see that round ball of grass?' It was the size of a football, or bigger, lying on the ground in the sunshine not far from the entrance to the sett. 'A badger's rolled that up to dry. In the evening time he'll come out and take it down into his bed – he goes down backwards, holding it between his back legs and steering with his front legs. They're making a lot of fresh bedding now, because in a week or two their cubs are going to be born.' This is why I knew it was urgent to get on with putting up my hide, so that I wouldn't disturb the cubs later. They're very small and delicate when they're first born, deep underground, and the mother is very nervous and shy. It would be three months before the badger cubs would be big enough to come out into the wide world for the first time.

Tawny owl in Brian and Maureen Letherby's garden shed

Wildlife will sometimes hide very close to humans in the winter. Outside my house there's a rowan tree, and one late afternoon in December as I drew up there with my truck and the small arched trailer shack I use at the Christmas fairs where I sell my films, I noticed two little birds sitting on a bare branch. They were jenny wrens, and when I went indoors and looked out of the window I saw one fly straight in under the arched, open roof of my trailer. I saw that he'd been waiting for me to come back, so that he could go to his roosting place; and I realised that he must be roosting there every night, underneath the shelter of the roof and away from the cold.

Small birds are quickly killed by the winter cold; and the wrens being almost our smallest bird – only the goldcrest is smaller – they need to keep as warm as they can. One cold winter day I watched a whole wren family, two parents and five grown-up youngsters, as they all piled into same nesting box in the garden, one after the other, until all seven of them had gone in for a cosy night out of the wind. It must have been a squeeze, but at least it was warm.

Food makes a big difference to the small birds in winter. February can be their worst month, with an extra cold spell just when the spring seems ready to burst through. Many people in the countryside still keep the old habit of putting out food for them in the cold weather. Some good peanuts or bird food, a cooked meaty bone hung up in a tree, or even some old dried bread will make all the difference.

When we first built the new badger hide at Twitchen, there was very little bird life in the oak woods there, except for a tawny owl calling across the dark winter valley. But I hung up bird feeders at the new hide, some high in the trees, others nearer the ground, and I kept them topped up with peanuts; and within a few weeks I was beginning to get good results. On one day at the hide at the end of February I saw 18 blue tits, 10 great tits, 5 cock chaffinches, 2 hedge sparrows, 2 robins, 2 blackbirds, a goldfinch, a marsh tit and a coal tit, and a pair of great spotted woodpeckers. It just shows how, by feeding, you can bring the birds from a long way away.

Marsh tit on peanuts at my new hide

Great spotted woodpecker at my hide

I was extra pleased to see the marsh tit. It isn't often seen, and when it's feeding on nuts during the winter months it's often taken for a blackcap. The difference is that the marsh tit has a black spot under his beak, and the blackcap is lighter in feathers, with a rounder cap.

Having the hide helps me film the birds, but out on the moor there's plenty to see as well. The bullfinches, the males with their bright red breasts, flock on the bramble seeds; and up above, you might be lucky and see the sparrowhawk hovering in the sky, or the buzzard circling high up. Fieldfares and redwings flock, and down in the valley you might see the songthrush, who was once common, though now he's rare. The songthrush is hard to tell apart from quite a few other birds: something bigger than the blackbird, he's speckled all over like the mistle thrush, and quite like the redwing in appearance except that he doesn't have the redwing's red flash under his wing.

Driving along the lanes in February, I'll often come across two cock pheasants fighting for territory in the road, ready for spring; or I'll spot a pair of herons getting ready for nesting. Herons lay their eggs in late February; but the earliest of all the birds to nest is the raven, our biggest black bird. If you're on the moor in January you might spot their big nest of sticks, high in the top of a tall tree or stuck on top of an electric pylon. Exmoor might be deep in snow, but the raven's getting on with the job. He's a protected bird, which mainly feeds on small mammals; but he's also the farmer's worst enemy when he pecks out the eyes of the newborn lambs in early spring.

In the winter I like to go rock fishing with my sons Stuart and Craig at Watermouth on the north coast. In the bitter easterly winds they'll wear wet suits, with whistles round their necks in case they're washed off the rocks, and they use beach casters, casting out a hundred yards into the sea.

It was something I used to do with them years ago, when they were boys; but now I'm older, I just like to go and watch with the family. We have to climb down over the rocks and find a sheltered place to see it all happening. These wild, wet days are good to see, with high, rough seas and wind blowing over the tops of the waves, making white horses far out on the water. The birds like them too: the black-backed gulls ride the waves and fish for themselves. There are black-headed gulls as well, and on the shore the smaller rock pipits, birds which live only on the coast, busily turning over sand and stones. As the light fades the boys will light a Tilley lamp and carry on, attaching little red reflectors to the tips of the rods so that they can see when they get a bite. Many times they'll fish the tide in. If they've done well we might bring back a couple of whiting, white-fleshed fish that we sprinkle with flour in the old-fashioned way, and then fry. I don't think anything could taste nicer.

Winter is a good time to see the sea birds which migrate to Devon's shores from colder parts of the world. At Fremington, on the estuary of the River Taw near Barnstaple, there's an RSPB bird sanctuary, where I went with the HTV film crew in the winter of 2001. I was surprised by the number of birds: dunlin, black-and-white oyster-catchers with long red legs; Canada geese, golden plover, and teal, bright green, very attractive birds with a dark band through the eye. I even saw four hen harriers, gliding low just above the ground.

While we were setting up for filming, we met a man who'd been coming to the same spot for fifty years. 'I never get tired of the birds here,' he told us. 'Have you seen the little egret? Exotic-looking. They come in to winter here. And the spoonbills have migrated here from Holland for the winter. You don't see them very often.' Like the little egrets, the spoonbills are white; and I know they're very unusual. There were five of them, but they were a long way out. 'What are my chances of filming them if I get closer?' I asked the crew. It was worth a try; but I knew that if I just walked out onto the sand they'd all fly away. So I decided to stalk them.

I crept out alongside the mud flats by a clay bank, through the reed beds, dressed in my usual camouflage gear. Stalking out on the open coast is difficult: you don't get much to hide in. But the late afternoon sun was very bright towards the birds, and I was in the shadow as I crept along the bank keeping my head down, so at least I was a little bit hidden. Anyway, it worked: I got so close to them that I could clearly see their spoons – the five-inch-long bills that give them their name – and I got some good shots of them cleaning themselves and dabbling in the sand. I couldn't have been more than 20 yards away from them: the film crew were amazed. In the end a man came with his dog and frightened the birds away; but that meant I could film the birds in flight too. What a thrill. On the way back from the marshes, in the dark, a barn owl flew right over us. It was a fantastic day, and I wouldn't have missed it for anything.

Winter on Exmoor is when we have all the whist drives in the villages, and people get together to raise money to keep things going on, from the staghounds and foxhounds to the village halls. Community events are very important to Exmoor people, and raising money is all part of it. In Bishops Nympton the Millennium Group in the year 2000 raised enough money with whist drives, bingo and social events to keep the church lit all year. It was winter when Dennis and Fran Gunn got a gang together to dig trenches for the cables, and because it meant digging around the church we had to call in archaeologists to check the ground. We weren't very surprised when they found medieval tiles under our trenches. Our village church has been there for a very long time.

Winter is a time for the pub, too, for skittles and friendly chats while the weather howls outside the door. My local is the King's Crow down in the village, and it does actually have a real crow inside – except that it's a jackdaw. The pub is the home of Paul and Roma, along with Jacko, a big black bird who lives in a cage by the bar and takes a great interest in all the customers.

Jacko arrived about 18 months ago, when one day Paul the landlord heard a tapping noise from inside the chimney. In our village nearly every chimney pot has a jackdaw's nest in it. Jackdaws love to use buildings for their nests, and they seem to like chimney pots especially. It can be a problem when people want to have their chimneys swept: even wire mesh across the top doesn't really keep them out, so you have to be careful what time of year you choose to do the sweeping, so as not to disturb the birds.

The nests are very big and straggly, built out of sticks; but inside they're neat and soft, carefully made and lined with sheep's wool. I've even seen jackdaws pitching down on Bambi's back and tugging at her rough coat, filling their beaks with her hair to line their nests with. Sadly, the baby birds often come to grief when they're beginning to fly. That was what had happened at the King's Crow: instead of flying away, the young bird had fallen down the chimney and couldn't get out.

Paul got Brian Chapman to help, and together they rescued the little bird by opening up the hatch underneath the fireplace. He was only a baby, so when they'd cleaned him up Paul and Roma left him outside on the bird table, hoping that his parents would come and feed him. But when no parent came they took him in themselves and reared him as a pet, feeding him on catfood and giving him a big cage by the bar.

Winter fields with snow thawing

Now that he's full grown, Jacko's very tame. He enjoys a drink of beer, and if you offer him your pint he'll often take a few sips. Sometimes Paul and Roma let him out, and he'll fly round the room and fetch up perched on the staghorns on the wall. Their pretty little black rescue dog with the curly face is jealous of Jacko, though; if you go in and say hello to Jacko and ignore him, he barks. It's quite a menagerie at the King's Crow. Everybody likes the bird and the dog.

The funniest thing about Jacko is his cleverness with money. If you give him a five-pence piece, he'll tap it on the floor of his cage to check it's real, and then he'll put it in his drinking pot, which he uses as a money box. And he's sharp and quick: you can't take it back once he's got it. He collects quite a lot of money that way, which Paul and Roma give to charity.

Most people know that jackdaws are famous for liking shiny objects, and they do have a habit of collecting them in their nests. And jackdaws especially are easily tamed. Years ago there was a jackdaw which used to live in a tree outside our house in High Bray. If my mum whistled to him, he would fly down and go right into the kitchen to drink from the tap. He appreciated the newly installed running water as much as we did.

Outside in the frozen fields, January is the mating season for the fox. If you go out and walk over the frosty moors and farmlands in the evenings or very early in the morning, you might hear them calling, with short, sharp, high-pitched barks, right across the moor. There are plenty of foxes, and it's not hard to find their dens – though, as with deer, if you're watching them you have to have the wind towards you. A dog fox will come back to mate with the same vixen year after year.

In winter, when they have to search further for food, it's easier to see foxes than in the summer time. They'll be crossing the road or running down into a wood, and their red coats and the white tip on the end of their tail are easy to spot against snow or frost. If snow is lying on the ground you can tell where a fox has been from his prints, which always form one straight line on the snow.

The fox will take anything to eat that he can get in winter, including a chicken or duck, or a pheasant poult. He can be very nimble. One snowy day I watched a fox lying in the snow, eyeing a blackbird sitting on a branch overhead. Even though it was three feet off the ground, he suddenly leapt into the air and snatched the bird right off the branch before it even had a chance to open its wings. Then he lay down again and ate it.

Winter can be a good time for taking fish, too. Years ago, five of us decided one night to go out to Landacre Bridge to take some salmon; so we all piled into a van, and off we went carrying a light to help us catch the fish. You aim the light onto the fish in the water; then, as you bring the beam into the bank, the fish will follow it – and if you're lucky, that's when you can catch him.

Landacre Bridge is high up on the moors, and it's often colder there than down in the valleys below. On that night there was a deep frost, and as we were fishing it started to snow. At first we hung on, hoping just to get a few more salmon. There were five of us, and we didn't have much of a catch. We'd been aiming at ten salmon, two each; but in the end, as the snow got thicker and heavier and the night wore on, we decided to call it a day at nine.

It was getting on for midnight as we started walking back up the hill through the snow to where our van was parked, carrying our fish. An Exmoor blizzard can white you out in seconds, and now the snow was falling fast. The further up the hill we went, the deeper it got, and we weren't surprised to find the van half-buried. We were stuck: we knew that it would never start. The only thing we could do was to leave it behind and walk all the way home, 12 miles across the moors.

But the fish was a problem. We couldn't take it with us; nine salmon are a lot to carry through a blizzard; and they were very big and obvious. Then someone had a bright idea. 'Why don't we bury them in the snow?' he said. 'They'll keep until we can come back and get them.' It seemed the best thing to do. There was a gutter in the road beside the van where the water runs off the moor, so we cleaned the snow out of it and buried the fish in, packed them round with snow, and set out across the moors for home.

Many travellers have been caught on Exmoor in snowstorms, and we knew we'd have a hard job to walk home through the blizzard that night. We laughed and joked as we walked along, but marching in the pitch darkness through the deep snow was tiring, with the wind-driven snow stinging our faces; and every step was getting harder. An hour or two later we stopped at a farm near Sandy Way pub, where we knocked on the door to ask if we could stay the night. My brother-in-law's long curly hair was frozen solid by now, and it rang like jingle bells as we knocked.

The farmer opened the door and looked at us doubtfully. You could see he wasn't keen on taking in the five of us in the middle of the night. On the other hand, he couldn't very well turn us off into that rough weather. He had a struggle to know what to say. 'Well, you can sleep in the cowshed with the cows if you like,' he said finally.

A frosty morning at Landacre

We didn't fancy that. 'No, we think we'll carry on, then,' we said, and walked on through the wind, with the snow pelting down.

By now the moor was looking like the North Pole, with drifts nearly as high as the telegraph wires, and we were going slower and slower as we struggled through each one and the hours went by. It was all too slow for Ted, who decided he'd get on better if he went on ahead on his own. A few miles up the road we found him curled up in a big snowdrift not very far from home at Pinkham's Corner, nearly asleep. I dragged him to his feet. 'Get up, Ted, you've got to get up,' I shouted, pulling him along. We knew that if we left him there he could have easily frozen to death.

Though our eyebrows were frozen solid and our hair was rattling with icicles, by six a.m. we'd made it back home to Bishops Nympton. Our families were waiting for us: they'd been worried to death, and couldn't believe it when we walked in through the door. We were very lucky to get home that night.

The blizzard was the beginning of a big freeze on the moor which went on for many days. Three days later I had a phone call from my friend Barry. 'How about those salmon out there, Johnny?' he said. He sounded very keen. I told him he could have them all if he wanted them; and five days later he went back and collected them, still frozen solid, and very fresh. The rest of us didn't mind. We'd had enough of the river, the salmon and the moor to last us for a good while.

Barle valley near Hawkridge

Sometimes, instead of snow, December brings heavy rains which fill the rivers bank-high. One rainy, cold day in early December I drove through the shallow river at Tarr Steps and up Winsford Hill to Landacre Bridge on the Barle, because I wanted to see how the salmon were getting on. All I saw at first were two salmon works, but no fish. So I put my camera away in the van and walked along, meaning to look along the bank a bit further on; and I hadn't gone 15 yards when suddenly I saw an otter jump out of the water, run along the river bank and then disappear again.

I only wished that I had my camera. I ran back to the truck to grab it, but it was too late. Otters travel far and wide, and I knew he might never come back. When I went back to the bank where I'd seen him, I did find his tracks on the sand, though they're hard to spot: the otter has tracks the same size as a badger's, and although he has webbed feet, often the webs don't show up on the sand.

I spent more than an hour by the Barle, hoping to see him again. There was spraint, otter droppings, on the sandbank, and I knew that his holt would be somewhere thereabouts, either in a big hole in a riverbank or else in an old moot by the river. As I watched I heard a dipper's high-pitched call, and one flew past very fast. He's a chubby little bird with a white throat, a little smaller than a blackbird, and he likes to nest in a moot as well, or underneath a bank or bridge. He builds a nest like a wren's, but bigger, a mossy ball with a hole near the top, about the size of a child's football. The dipper landed on a stone in the river and dipped up and down, looking for minnows; then he suddenly dived right underneath the water. They can stay underwater a long time, and I've often seen them come up with a fish and knock it against a stone to kill it.

I walked on through some rushes, when all at once I came upon a buzzard hawk busily eating a dead salmon on the riverbank. And then I understood the full story. The otter had taken advantage of the full waters in the rain to help himself to a good salmon. He'd dragged it onto the bank to eat, and then something disturbed him and he ran away, and now the buzzard was finishing off his meal. Once again, I'd arrived too late to film him. But I still hope that someday I shall manage it.

Though winter may look dead, there's life stirring underneath the earth. One fine cold winter's day I was at Rose Ash, working on a grave with my son, when three feet down we came upon a little burrow containing quite a number of

Roe doe near Bishops Nympton and roe buck in velvet

slow-worms, all twined up together. The slow-worm looks like a snake, but he's really a legless lizard, and can't bite or sting. He's pretty to look at, of a silvery colour, but he's also quite shy; and when he hibernates he'll dig right down into the earth to find a spot to sleep out the winter. These were young slow-worms: the biggest were only eight inches long, and there were some no longer than four inches.

They were very sleepy, as you'd expect. I lifted them and put them under the heaped stuff at the side of the grave; then when we'd finished we buried them at a depth of three feet again, being careful not to damage them. They would have plenty of time to wake before the spring.

Some shy animals are easier to spot in winter. One of these is the roe deer, which hides among the trees in summer, but in winter, with the trees bare, it's much easier to see him. In January the buck is in velvet, and growing his antlers, and he eats a lot of leaves, shoots, roots and dried-up plants, just as the red deer do. You can tell if a roe deer has been in the woods by his very, tiny, shiny droppings. The leaves will be disturbed in a circle where he's been lying, and there'll be a few little needle-like, pale brown hairs on the ground.

Once I came across quite a number of roe tracks in the woods. The roe stag leaves a hoof mark with a wider slot than the hind or calf, where its toes are spread out; and I could tell from the tracks that there were two hinds and a buck here.

So I went further very carefully and soon saw the three of them a safe distance away. I didn't waste any time getting my shots. They soon ran away.

Although winter seems dead, many creatures are preparing for spring in their own way. Here in the South-West the frogs start spawning as early as January, though in other parts of the country it's later; and the toads soon follow. When we were children we loved to collect the frog's soft piles of dotted jelly, and the

Toad in early spring

Stream running through Snowdrop Valley

toad's long jelly strands with dots following each other, and take them home to hatch into tadpoles.

The frog is the first to mate. When the season's upon him, the outside toe on the front feet of the male swells up so that he can grab hold of the female and hold on. And hold on they do. One year I filmed 14 males piled up on one female, all clutched together in a big ball, rolling over and over and croaking their loud, sharp croak. When you hear it you know that, even though it might be cold and dark, the frogs are busy out there in the freezing water.

The toad is more solitary and private. He lives on grassland most of the time, feeding on insects and slugs and hibernating under a big stone or a lump of wood, crawling rather than hopping. You'll often find him in the garden, cold and clammy as though he's dead. It's best to leave him alone: chances are, he'll wake when the weather warms up, and eat your garden pests.

For the mating season, though, the toad seeks out water just like the frog. They're easy to tell apart – our frogs are yellowy with black spots, whereas the toad is a darker colour, somewhat bigger, and with a rougher skin. Both of them appreciate a good, still, clean pond for spawning.

Although winter seems so dead and cold, by February the lambs' tails are out in the valleys on the hazels, and the snowdrops are springing up by the river banks where the badgers live. A couple of weeks later they'll all be in bloom in the sheltered valleys and churchyards across Exmoor. Every year, like many people, we visit Snowdrop Valley, a famous beauty spot between Exford and Wheddon Cross where the snowdrops carpet the ground along the river banks. So many people love it there that cars have to park a little way up, and you have to catch a minibus down to the site. But when you get down into the valley, the sight of the millions of flowers there can take your breath away.

In Snowdrop Valley

Although it's still winter, by mid-February there are primroses beginning to flower along the high banks, and even on dry, frosty days you see the pussy-willow springing in the hedges. This is the time of year when I once brought a rooster home in a haversack on my back.

There was a time during my lumberjack days when we kept hens in the back garden, for their prettiness and their eggs. We had all sorts: Rhode Island reds, bantams, mallard and Aylesbury ducks and pheasants. One year I thought we'd try to breed up some chickens ourselves from the eggs my birds at home were laying, so I started to look out for a rooster. I was working for a firm called Bakers at the time, going round the countryside taking down diseased elm trees. One day they sent me to a smallholding near Taunton to take down a big tree, and I was pleased to see that there were several roosters in the yard.

'I wouldn't mind having one of those roosters,' I said to the farmer. He agreed to let me have one; but then there was the problem of how to get it home. In those days I used to ride a motorbike, which was much cheaper to run than a car, and I would carry my dinner tin in a haversack on my back. 'Let me try putting him in my haversack, and see how he likes it,' I suggested. So we wedged him in beside the dinner tin, in such a way that he couldn't move his body and his head was sticking out looking over my shoulder at the road ahead. He seemed to be

Squirrels in my mum's garden

quite comfortable on my back; and he didn't crow once all the way down the M5.

But he did the job with the hens, and soon we were pleased to see them getting broody. When the chicks hatched out we hoped they'd be good layers. We didn't bargain for them turning out to be mostly roosters.

As the young roosters grew, they started crowing every morning; which, since there were eight of them, made quite a noise. This went on for some months, until in the end I thought I'd better be sensible. They couldn't lay eggs, so we should eat them. For a long time I didn't have the heart to kill them; but in the end I did it, cleaned them, plucked them and put them in the freezer.

Then came another problem. None of us wanted to take them out and cook them. Every time one came up to the top of the freezer, I'd put it down again at the bottom. We'd petted and played with those roosters, and it just wasn't in me to eat them.

This went on for more than a year, until in the end I told my neighbour Mary about my problem. 'Eight roosters, Mary, and we can't eat any of them,' I said.

'Well, I'll have them then, Johnny, I don't mind,' she laughed. So that was where they ended up – on Mary's dinner table.

As well as chickens I used to keep ferrets for rabbiting. We handled them easily, but a ferret will bite someone it doesn't know viciously. Once, when we were out for the day, one of them escaped and ran for the lane below our house, where it caught the eye of a passing lady. Ferrets are pretty little things, with their smooth, long bodies and pointed faces, but it's a mistake to pet them, as she quickly found out. As she brought it up to her face, it turned its head and bit her on the ear so hard that she had to go to hospital for an anti-tetanus jab. She kept well away from ferrets after that.

Winter is when the squirels eat the acorns that they've worked hard all autumn to gather. But they'll eat other things too. My mother loves feeding the birds, and because she lives right beside a wood she also gets a lot of squirrels, so she also has a proper squirrel feeding box in her garden. The squirrels are her friends, and it's comical to see how they'll open the box by tilting the lid up with their head, reach in and takes a nut, and sit on the bird table to eat it. Often mum will see two or three at a time helping themselves to the nut feast. My mum's getting on in years now, but she loves the wildlife still.

This woodmouse had a lucky escape

Winter is a time when digging graves is wet and heavy work; but there's wildlife everywhere, even in the grave. Once I was working in South Molton churchyard. I'd finished the digging, and I was just packing up when I saw a little wood mouse trapped right in the corner of the pit down below, looking at me and hardly daring to move.

Luckily I had my camera with me. I filmed it, and then lifted it gently out of the grave and let it run across the grass to freedom. I don't know where it went after that, but that little mouse was very lucky that I was there. It would live to run another day.

WESTERN DAILY PRESS

LAST THOUGHTS

Exmoor's beauty is very old. My country has been here a long time, and it's a comfort to think that it'll still be here, with its seasons and its creatures, long after I've gone. When I dig a grave in a country graveyard, in the old way, with a pick and shovel and listening to the birds, I feel peaceful as I work. They always say that the best people are in the ground. Because they don't argue with you, do they? They're lovely people. The way I look at it, death is a part of life; and there's never a grave I dig without a robin coming to join me.

For 50 years on and off I've dug graves within a 20-mile radius of Bishop's Nympton. In time I took over from my dad as the local gravedigger, and I've worked in most of the Exmoor churchyards over the years: my home church of High Bray, South Molton, Rose Ash, East and West Anstey, Charles, Chorley,

Chumleigh, Chillhampton, where I was confirmed as a boy by the bishop, George Nympton, Bishops Nympton, Kings Nympton, Dulverton, Brushford, Molland, Simonsbath and Exford. It's no wonder that I get aches and creaks sometimes, now that I'm getting older. Digging graves is a tough job, and I'm lucky that my sons and some of my mates help me. Plenty of the lads in the village have had a go at giving me a hand at one time or another; but most don't come back a second time.

Many times I've had to dig a grave for a friend or a relative. I've laid to rest many people I know, including my own father, when his time came. I've even had people die and put in their will that they want their grave dug by Johnny Kingdom.

When I'm doing a job I always say to myself, well, I'm doing a kind deed for the person in the coffin. I don't think I've ever buried someone without saying something to them in my heart. If I can, I'll ask the family for permission to see the dead person before they're laid to rest and buried, so that I can say goodbye. Death is so final.

The years of our lives pass quickly by, and you never know what's round the corner. Since the day of my terrible accident, life has changed for me. I've learnt how to film wildlife, and I'm learning more every day. I've produced 26 wildlife videos of my own, and a two-hour audio tape, and I've appeared on breakfast TV, documentaries and children's TV, for BBC, YTV, HTV and Channel 4. For the last seven years I've been making series and documentaries for HTV about Exmoor and Somerset wildlife with Available Light Productions in Bristol, which has taken me to some interesting places and led me to meet some lovely people. Recently I've started working with the writer Christina Zaba, to create a weekly wildlife page in the Western Daily Press, and now this book. Around Exmoor many people know me, and I'm often honoured by being asked to open local fetes, give talks and film shows, or help with school or charity events. I've loved showing people what the animals are really like, and it's always good to see how many people do care.

In my time I've reared deer and chickens, mice and ferrets and sheep, dogs and cats, owls and buzzards. I've built three hides, and trained wild badgers to run up and down ladders and walkways, and turn big wheels with peanuts inside; I've rescued nests and followed foxes and stags, badgers and birds. You could say I'm a wildlife man.

Through the hours and hours I've spent on my own lying down on the wet ground on my stomach to watch the animals, I've understood many things. I've seen how they live and survive, I've watched them play and eat and sleep. I've let them come to me in their own way, in their own world. This is how I've got to know them.

People sometimes laugh at me for spending time up in the trees. 'What are you doing that for, Johnny? That bloke, he's mad,' they'll say. But it's surprising what you can see from the top of a tree. If you wait there long enough, and watch

JONATHAN HAWES

Richard Taylor-Jones of Available Light Productions filming me for the new HTV series

carefully, you'll see the true story of the wildlife, what it's really like. Not many people will take the time to do it.

Sitting in trees isn't very comfortable; and that's why I like to build a hide off the ground, where I can sit more easily and just wait. It's like watching a story unfold: you don't know what you're going to see next. Maybe a deer will come along, or a woodpecker or fox; or, if it's evening time, you might see a badger. To see the wildlife in its own natural way of living is beautiful. When you manage to film something well it gives you a hell of a kick; there's something that goes right through your body at that moment. If you watch wildlife with a good heart, there's such a joy in it. To me it's the best kind of relaxation there is.

Like all my family, I'm big in belief. When anything goes wrong in my life I pray to the Lord for help, and it's surprising what results I get. There is always a result there, as I've seen many times. Often when I'm in a graveyard I'll walk round and read the tombstones, and think about who lies beneath. I've buried some of my old class at school, and I'll stand at the grave of my friend, and talk to him in my heart. You're not really gone, I'll think. I don't think anyone can die and just be forgotten. We'll all meet again in another world: I'm sure of that.

People who have lost loved ones will often come to me at the graveside to talk. I always try to reassure them if I can. 'You'll see them again one day, have no fear,' I'll say. The hardest thing is burying little children. It hurts me so much to think of a life so soon over. Many people know how it feels to lose a child from

RICHARD TAYLOR JONES

With my mum

the family; my own three nephews died, two of them when they were just 3 and 8 years old. Losing a child is one of the greatest sorrows there is, and it's hard to understand what the Lord means by it. But there's a saying, that from the moment you're born your days are numbered; and I think it's true.

Once I was at my front door, looking towards the cemetery where a funeral was ending. I knew I had to go down and bury a child who had died, and I didn't want to go. It was only a small grave, two and a half feet deep; my son had helped me dig it. But I knew that it would be difficult to be there, on my own, filling in the earth over that coffin. The family lived not far from my own village, and I knew how much they'd loved the young baby that they'd lost.

I knew the undertaker was waiting, so I began to walk to the churchyard. As I approached, I could see that the parents of the child were there waiting for me too. They'd been crying. 'Hello, Johnny,' said the father. 'I knew it would be you. I want you to look after our little daughter.' When I saw that little coffin I broke my heart. Every shovelful I put into that grave I did with my bare hands. 'One day you will join this little baby – that's my belief,' I said to the parents. The spirit does lift up to another place when we pass on, I think; and I know that we've all got to go there in the end.

Sorrow doesn't pass anybody by in this world. My mum is 86 years old, and at the moment she has cancer. It's hard to think that we might lose her, though she's strong in belief, taking everything in her stride, and she still has a smile for everybody. That's why this book is dedicated to her, for all the kind things she's done for all of us.

I'm very lucky to have a strong family, with all of us still living in the Exmoor area. Although our dad's passed on now, our mum is still with us. I've got a lovely wife who I think the world of, and who after nearly 40 years with me deserves at least three gold medals. I've got my two sons, Stuart and his wife Sue, Craig and his partner Jane, and my two beautiful granddaughters Louise and Roxy, not forgetting Roxy's mum Gabrielle. My five sisters and their families all live within fifteen miles of us, and as well as that I've got my wife's family, especially my mother-in-law, a lovely person who lives in our village. My sisters and I are great friends, and we're always ringing one another up. I know I've been a rogue in my time, but I've never harmed anyone; and they're proud of all I've done.

A lot of people get things handed down to them through their families. In our lives that didn't happen: we've had to try hard for everything. But we've always had each other, and we've always had our home.

Exmoor is a lovely place, and my hope is that it will be kept that way, that people won't destroy our way of living, and that they'll take good care of it and all its creatures in the years to come, so that others in the future will learn to appreciate the wildlife, just as I have. As I see it, we're all here together, and our time is too short to waste. I think maybe if more people thought like that, things would go more smoothly in the world.

Strolling on the moor with Julie